How to Talk to Your Lawyer

How to

TALK

to Your

LAWYER

So you can get the results YOU want!

- ► 25+ Savvy Client Tips
- ► Templates to keep you involved and organized
- ► Insiders' tips that demystify the practice of law
- ► A Glossary of legal terms for non-lawyers

Another creative
business tool from

RIGHTBRAIN
Ventures

Elura Nanos, Esq.
Michele Sileo, Esq.

Acknowledgements

Thanks, hugs, and general shout-outs to . . .

Libby Ladu, for believing that we are special enough to collaborate with; Nell Merlino and the Count Me In team, for inspiring us to talk slower, work harder, and dream bigger; Phil Mittleman, who generously read and commented on early drafts; Emily Merowitz Tedeschi, for knowing a lot more than two know-it-alls knew; Marla, for giving us permission to be our loudmouthed selves; all our family members, friends, and neighbors, for coming through with the childcare necessary to make this book a reality; our children, for taking naps, playing video games, and watching television as we drafted our manuscript; our husbands, for always seeming to know just how to talk to the lawyers in their own houses; New York Law School, for providing fertile ground in which true friendship can blossom; and the general legal community, for giving us an endless supply of work by making law as confusing as possible.

Table of Contents

Introduction

Why aren't lawyers afraid of automation taking over their professions? *No one would build a robot to do nothing.*

What do you get when you cross The Godfather with a lawyer? *An offer you can't understand.*

What's the difference between a lawyer and a herd of buffalo? *The lawyer charges more.*

We've heard the jokes. We've endured the jokes. On occasion, we've even made the jokes. Lawyers seem to be everyone's favorite necessary evil, which makes them a fabulous punchline, time and again. We also know that behind all the jokes, there's, well, something. It's not quite love. It's not quite respect. It's not quite fear. But it's something that the writers of Law & Order have managed to entertain audiences with for over two decades.

For a lot of people, their lawyer is the *ringer* of their team. Your lawyer is your ace-in-the-hole, ready to hit one out of the park whenever it's really important. There's just nothing better than having the ability to shout "I'M CALLING MY LAWYER" knowing that there's a bulldog-for-hire in your corner. But that same ringer can strike fear in your own heart – even though he works for you! At any moment, your ace's legal bill can come rocketing across your desk, with all the muscle that once backed you – behind *it*. Powerless, you succumb to your own doubts, and quickly pay your bill . . . no questions asked.

We think that it's high time that you, the clients, get some power and take charge of the attorney-client relationship. For over a decade, we've experienced first hand the complexities and subtleties of the lawyer-client relationship. We've represented big clients (like the City of New York and Commerce Bank) and small clients (like Michele's Uncle Jerry and Elura's friend Rocco). Our business is built on our ability to help law students remain human on their way to passing the bar. So we know that on the outside, your attorney may seem über-confident, sleekly professional and always in charge. But underneath, he or she is an actual person with his or her own strengths and (dare we say it?) weaknesses.

We understand why clients often are frustrated with their lawyers. And we've seen clients do things to unwittingly sabotage their own relationship with counsel. We get it. So we're going to give you information from the inside so that you get it too.

Does this mean we're turncoats? Not at all. We are proud to be lawyers and we are proud to associate with many brilliant, ethical, creative, and talented fellow members of the bar. They are out there, we promise! We just know that the attorney-client relationship sometimes needs some tweaking. Think of this book as Dorothy's ruby slippers. You've always had the power – you just didn't know how to use it. With some good advice from those of us who've been on the other side of the counsel table, you'll be prepared to have a truly rewarding relationship with your own attorney. Just click your heels (and read this book)!

CHAPTER 1

What Lawyers DON'T Know and What You Need to Know

We know this sounds a little crazy, but in law school, people don't learn how to be good lawyers. Yes, they learn the law. They take courses in legal history, important case precedents, legal theory and complex legal concepts. They learn to analyze, hypothesize, and synthesize. And they learn to write, think, and talk *like lawyers* (which sometimes, apparently means forgetting how to think or talk like normal humans)! But they don't actually learn the nuts and bolts of the practice of law – like which papers go with which lawsuits, or which words have to go on which contracts. And, they *definitely* don't learn how to calm down a client who is stressed out because his landlord locked him out . . . or because he's never heard the words "due diligence" before and is sure that it's something very scary.

Don't tell Harvard, but law school is a lot like the classroom part of Driver's Ed. You have to attend to learn the rules and get your license. But it doesn't really teach you what it feels like to get behind the wheel. Medical students do get actual clinical training. The chronology goes a little like this: first, doctors-to-be learn from books. Then, they work on dead people. Then, they practice working on live people under the supervision of experienced doctors. And finally, when they're good and ready, they are launched into the world with their white coats and stethoscopes. Law students, on the other hand, get all the way to their J. D. s without ever seeing a real client, dead *or* alive.

So how do lawyers learn the job of actually being lawyers? Most of the time, they learn by doing. Just like at any other job, colleagues and supervisors walk junior lawyers through the required day-to-day tasks.

And how do lawyers become good lawyers? Well, some never do! But most lawyers become good at certain things and gravitate toward the niches where they excel.

What does this system mean to you, as a client? It means that some lawyers will have a style with which you will feel comfortable, and will have experience that is relevant. *Some* is the key word here. There's a pretty wide variety out there, and not every lawyer is the lawyer for you. For example, you should expect that if your lawyer has worked at the Real Estate firm of Closem, Mortgagem & Foreclosem for thirty years, she probably has no idea how to file a sexual harassment lawsuit. If your lawyer has a background in taking corporate fat cats to court, he may not be the appropriate choice to negotiate a sensitive issue with a valued employee.

There are plenty of lawyers out there. Specialists, generalists, aggressive types, intellectual types, practical business-oriented advisors, and silver-tongued idealists. Some have lots of experience in limited areas; some have a little experience in a wide variety of practice areas. Some have been lawyers since the courthouse was built, and some are just starting out in the legal world. Some want to learn and some want to teach.

So, how do you choose? And once you pick one, how do you manage the lawyer-client relationship? How do you avoid those uncomfortable situations where you end up agreeing to pay for something you don't understand? How do you avoid unsatisfying outcomes? How do you ensure that no one will take advantage of you?

RELAX: You're the BOSS. You can call the shots. This little book is here to help you find the right fit and get the results you want from your lawyer.

CHAPTER 2

Letters for Lawyers: the Schooling Behind the Degrees

ere's how it all works. A law-school graduate receives a *Juris Doctorate* (J.D.), which means that he has completed all the courses required by his law school. A person with a J. D. knows a lot about law, and could be a professor or business advisor, but cannot actively practice law. To become a real, live lawyer, he must sit for the bar exam. Although "the bar exam" sounds very universal, it really isn't. Part of the bar is the same from state to state, and part of the bar is unique to each state. When someone passes the bar, he gets "admitted" to the state administering the exam. This is also known as becoming "licensed" to practice law. Only a person who is "admitted" may practice law, and being admitted to practice law in Kentucky doesn't mean he'll be able to practice law in Wyoming.

After being admitted, most lawyers put the letters "Esq." (as an abbreviation for Esquire) after their names. Unlike an abbreviation such as M. D. or D. O. or C. P. A., which is informative, the abbreviation Esq. really tells the reader nothing. There are no official rules for when "Esq." is allowed, nor does it denote any educational level, certification, or specialty. It's just a tradition. In ye days of olde, British male lawyers were called "Esquires" to clarify their social status. American lawyers (and now, even female lawyers) have held onto the tradition. Plus, it's no fun to have a monogrammed briefcase without extra letters following your name.

A very few lawyers get advanced law degrees, called L.L.M.s (Masters Degree in Law) or S.J.D.s (equivalent to a Ph.D. in Law). These are advanced academic degrees awarded in specialized fields, such as tax law or patent law. Don't be disappointed if your lawyer doesn't have any of these extra letters. It doesn't mean he's an underachiever. Hardly anyone has an L.L.M. or S.J.D.

A Doctor of Laws degree (L.L.D.) is an honorary degree, given to graduation speakers – they really have nothing to do with studying or practicing the law. This is good news for George W. Bush, who actually received an L.L.D. from Notre Dame in 2001, without having to crack a single book or learn a word of Latin.

We apologize. We know this stuff is a little dry. But you're the one becoming a savvy client ... a few paragraphs won't kill you.

Savvy Client Tip: **Learn what your lawyer should be doing, so that you can actively supervise his work.**

CHAPTER 3

What Happens From State to State?

Can a lawyer who is admitted in one state practice law in another state? Yes, sometimes. But there are a lot of variables. Because attorneys are licensed by the states in which they practice, they can practice law any way they want within that particular state. When lawyers want to practice outside their home states, things can become more complicated.

The bottom line? Some matters *must* be handled by an attorney who is licensed in a particular state, while some other matters *can* be handled by an out-of-state attorney.

Don't worry. It's not your problem to sort it all out. No lawyer wants to get involved in a project that exceeds the scope of his license. The best thing to do is simply ask your lawyer whether he is or isn't licensed to handle your matter. Trust us. He'll know the answer.

CHAPTER 4

When Do You Need a Lawyer?

This book is meant to be a resource for you as you're dealing with choosing and working with a lawyer. But we know that many of you are stuck at a more preliminary question: "Do I *need* a lawyer?"

The truth is that we really, *really* wish we could answer that question for you in a way that would satisfy you as a reader. It would be great if we could give you a little flowchart that you could follow right to "Congratulations! You don't need to hire a lawyer!" or "Go directly to the yellow pages and hire a lawyer before passing GO."

But it's a little more complicated than that.

As lawyers, we're on the hook for any legal advice we give you. If we shared an elevator ride with you, listened to your legal woes, and gave you thirty-seconds of advice that turned out to be incorrect, we could be liable for professional malpractice even if you never paid us a dime. Most professionals (whether lawyers, doctors and dentists, or roofers, plumbers, and painters) advise people about only the *safest* course of action. You'd never hear from your cardiologist, "You know, Horace, you're pretty slim, so smoking a pack a day probably won't kill you." You'd never hear a plumber say, "Well, Francine, you're pretty handy. Here's a book on toilets. Good luck!" Similarly, you'll never hear a lawyer say, "Edna, I think you're kinda smart – you can probably draft your will on your own. " That's the thing about professionals – we *always* believe we'd do a better job than a non-professional. Lawyers are no exception. And we'd never want to be the person who advised you to handle something yourself, only to find out later that do-it-yourself advice landed you in legal hot water.

But none of this means that you *can't* handle simple legal matters on your own. As lawyers, we're experts in knowing what lawyers do. We're not experts in knowing what non-lawyers might be able to do if they really applied themselves. So while we won't make the decision for you, we can give you some guidelines to follow to help you make the best decision for yourself.

WHEN SHOULD YOU HIRE A LAWYER?

1. **If you are being sued, hire a lawyer.** Take those scary papers that you've received and make sure to put them into a lawyer's hands within a few days. In fact, if you even suspect that you're going to be sued in the near future, hire a lawyer *now*. Lawyers can predict all sorts of consequences that non-lawyers may not foresee. Once a lawsuit has been started, the clock is ticking, and the court is involved. There are things that you need to do . . . now. And you probably have only a vague idea about what those things even are. This is a time to hire someone immediately. We got the point across, right?

2. **If you are suing someone in a big lawsuit, hire a lawyer.** What's a "big" lawsuit? Any case that isn't happening in small claims court. Anything that has a big dollar amount in dispute (use the term "big" for whatever it means to you personally). If you're suing someone for more than a few bucks, call a lawyer. Yes, you'll have to pay the lawyer. But it'll be worth it.

3. **If you are suing someone in a small lawsuit, maybe you can handle it yourself.** What's a "small" lawsuit? Any case that is in small claims court is . . . well . . . *small* (clever how they got that name, huh)? Some cases that are in other courts can also be small, such as eviction proceedings in housing court. If your case is a small one, then it's possible that you can handle it yourself, learn a little about the legal system, and save a few bucks by doing so.

4. **If nobody is suing anyone, but you are considering hiring a lawyer for some other purpose, then maybe you can do it yourself.** Make the decision here just as you would with home-improvement. Get a sense of the scope of the project. Learn what a professional would do to accomplish your goal. Evaluate the resources you have available to you. Create a realistic budget and timeline. Consider whether you want to do this yourself. Factor in the value of adding this particular skill into your repertoire. If all signs point to DIY, then you may be able to save a few bucks while learning about the law.

Why are we saying *"Maybe* you can handle it by yourself?" Because a lot of variables impact whether a decision to represent yourself in litigation would be a good one. Do-it-yourself can be a good option in law just as it is in home-improvement. (See Chapter 16 for more hints.) If you're good at it, then the results can be fantastic. If you're lousy at it, you'll end up with a big, annoying, expensive-to-fix mess.

Sometimes when people ask the question, "Do I NEED a lawyer" they really mean "How can I get what I need done as inexpensively as possible?" or "Do I need a lawyer NOW?"

To that, we say something that you're going to hate: it depends. There are certainly things you can do well on your own. And for things that you absolutely *need* a lawyer to accomplish properly, you should be smart about *how* and *when* you use your money. But let's make one thing clear: savvy clients don't find their lawyers (or their doctors or therapists or carpenters) in the discount bin. Lawyering up costs money. Savvy clients spend the right amount of money, get good representation, and are satisfied with their results.

There are also some reasonable alternatives to going straight to the law firm of Beau, Tye and Cuflinx. For example, **mediation** can provide a quicker and cheaper road to a divorce settlement than traditional litigation would. This probably isn't a good idea if your primary goal is making your soon-to-be-ex as miserable as possible … But if your main concern is saving money, check out some local mediators.

And don't forget that you can use non-legal professionals to get quite a bit accomplished. For example, a good business coach might help you choose the proper structure for your new business. And an accountant may be just the right person to explain the tax advantages of an L.L.C. versus those of a corporation.

CHAPTER 5

What Kinds of Lawyers Are There?

So there you are. You've accepted that you need to hire a lawyer, and now it's time to figure out exactly *what kind* of lawyer to hire. Figuring out the "what kind" can be incredibly daunting. And going to websites or the yellow pages can feel like reading the menu at a French restaurant. You know you're hungry. You know the menu is describing food. But the comprehension ends there. *Everything* sounds fancy, complex, and intimidating – and ultimately, you have very little idea what you're actually getting yourself into.

In an effort to ensure that you don't end up with the legal equivalent of a duck leg when what you wanted was a cup of coffee, we offer the following cast of characters:

Litigators: This group handles lawsuits and court appearances. These are the guys the best-selling novelists write about, because their work is aggressive, adversarial, and sometimes, high-profile. Whether you're the one suing or the one being sued, your lawyer is a litigator. There are several types of

Litigators. For example, **Trial law/commercial litigation/civil practice lawyers** are the Marines of the legal world. They are the smooth-talking, pinstripe-wearing, strategy-minded spotlight seekers of John Grisham fame. If you are involved in any kind of lawsuit in which the outcome will involve money (and not jail time), these are the people with whom you'll be working. Like lawsuits themselves, litigators come in many flavors. Some specialize in certain types of lawsuits, while others will handle anything that affects you or your business in any way. Regardless of your litigator's advertised specialty, you can be sure that he or she knows the rules of the game, and is well-versed in everything from judge's chambers to jury instructions.

Torts/Negligence/Personal Injury ("PI") lawyers are the guys who specialize in "woulda," "coulda" and "shoulda." If you've gotten hurt because someone somehow screwed up, you're calling a Plaintiff's Personal Injury Lawyer. If *you* are the screw-up, you're calling the PI defense bar.

Arbitration/Mediation: These days, many lawsuits and other matters, like divorce, are settled as a result of non-courtroom arbitration or mediation. Because this kind of resolution is more efficient and less expensive than regular, old litigation, this area of law is growing by the day.

Alternative Dispute Resolutions are typically handled by lawyers with litigation training, but their rates are lower. When there is a commercial dispute of some kind, you can bet that some kind of alternative dispute resolution is bound to be a choice – and often, a good one.

Transactional/Document-Drafting/General Advising: These are the guys that specialize in the "heretofores" and "notwithstandings." These lawyers draft the documents packed with jargon, and play pass-the-paper with other lawyers during closings and other deals. These guys are also the ones you can call when you have a quick question about how to do something within your business.

Advocates and other go-betweens: In today's society, many individuals need lawyers to represent them during outside-the-courtroom events. Lawyers with specialized knowledge often set up a practice as advocates for things like special education conferences, school board hearings, or employee disciplinary conferences. Lots of people feel more secure when going into a high-stakes situation with a lawyer, and lots of lawyers are happy to oblige.

Corporate: "Corporate Law" is a problematic expression, because it tends to be thrown around loosely within legal circles. Often, lawyers will say that they practice "corporate law" when their clients are...you guessed it . . . *corporations*. But that tidbit doesn't really help, because *McDonalds* is a corporation... and so is *Francine's Corner Store Tea Cozies*. Most "corporate law firms" have at least 100 lawyers, and are the Goliaths of the legal world. Most of their clients are large companies with deep pockets, and most of their work consists of major transactions (mergers, acquisitions, and other large-scale financial matters) and huge, complicated lawsuits. On the other hand, smaller firms and even solo practitioners may describe their practice area as "corporate law" when they simply mean that they specialize in setting up, advising, and representing small businesses. The bottom line: if you're considering hiring Carol the Corporate Lawyer, ask some questions to make sure that Carol usually handles matters just like the one your corporation has right now.

General Counsel/In-House Counsel: If you're reading this book, you probably won't be hiring these guys. These lawyers work for a business, not for a law firm. They do not take clients. Some in-house lawyers advise the business in different ways (think Tom Hagen's role in *The Godfather*). Others act like professional *clients* and hire "outside" law firms to handle legal matters. The in-house lawyer would supervise all legal work and then report to the business' non-lawyers on what's happening.

Real estate: You can be pretty confident that if you are buying, leasing, or renting any kind of property, a real estate lawyer is your man. Some Real Estate lawyers specialize only in residential matters, while others handle only commercial matters, and many do both. It is important to know that most real estate lawyers deal with transactional work (the "pass-the-paper" stuff) and not litigation (the "I'll-see-you-in-court" stuff). When things go bad, there are "real estate litigation" lawyers, but don't assume that the same guy will fill both roles.

Intellectual property or "IP": These are the lawyers who deal with patents, trademarks, and copyrights. If you've invented something, written a song, painted a picture, created a logo, developed a secret formula, or simply want to register your company's name, this is who you call. "Intellectual Property" refers to the area of law where someone owns something that isn't land and isn't physical, tangible stuff. There are lots of different reasons why you might need an IP lawyer, from registering your ownership right, to searching what others might already own, to handling lawsuits when someone copies or uses your stuff without authorization. IP tends to be a highly-specialized area of law, and lawyers who are IP specialists usually don't handle other kinds of legal matters. In fact, Patent Lawyers are extra fancy because they've taken a specialized bar exam in addition to the regular old bar. IP legal work often happens in a relatively small law firm, but still carries a big-firm price-tag.

Employment law: Employment lawyers are sometimes commercial litigators who are capable of handling cases related to the employer-employee relationship. Other times, employment lawyers devote their entire practice to assisting businesses in developing and maintaining legally sound employment policies.

General practice: This means the same thing in law as it does in medicine. Your general practice attorney may well be able to handle all of your legal needs. She probably routinely handles real-estate closings, uncontested divorces, simple contracts, traffic tickets, business incorporation and simple criminal cases. Lawyers with a general practice also usually have a wide network of specialists to whom they can refer you, or even collaborate with if your case falls outside their area of expertise.

Administrative law: "Administrative Law" refers to legal and "quasi-legal" issues that involve Administrative Agencies. Stay with us.... don't glaze over. Administrative Agencies are organizations that are created by the government, but that have their own internal legal system. Think capital letters. The IRS, DMV, EPA, FDA and TSA are all administrative agencies. Lawyers who specialize in administrative law are experts at handling legal or kinda-legal matters within these agencies. So for example, if you own a drug company and you need a lawyer to help you get FDA approval for the latest weight-loss pill, you'd go to an administrative lawyer. Two years from now, when your company is being sued because the pill ended up causing patients to grow extra toes, you'll go to a Commercial Litigator.

Bankruptcy: "Bankruptcy lawyers" come in several varieties. Some work with individuals and small businesses to advise them during a financial crisis, and to deal with corresponding paperwork when the client has chosen to file for bankruptcy. Others work with larger businesses, when "filing for bankruptcy" is an incredibly complex matter. Still others work on behalf of the court or various creditors to handle the monumental amount of administrative work that goes along with actually effectuating a bankruptcy filing.

Collections: When someone owes you money and isn't paying up, a "collections attorney" is someone you may want to call. Lawyers that specialize in collections matters can do a variety of things that'll help you get money out of your particular deadbeat. This can mean sending threatening letters, or negotiating payments with the deadbeat personally, filing the appropriate lawsuits, turning the verdicts from those lawsuits into actual cash, and even dealing with credit bureaus. Of course, you'll probably need to pay your collections lawyer a piece of what he collected on your behalf – but you can be sure that by using him, you'll likely get more out of your deadbeat than you ever could have gotten on your own.

Criminal Law: You know what we mean here. Turn on the television during prime time, any night of the week. You'll see actors who've perfected that frazzled-yet-heroic look bounding into courtrooms and delivering Oscarworthy speeches to rapt jurors. In real life, the courtrooms are much dustier, the lawyers are more rumpled, and the jurors are asleep – but other than that, it's just like TV.

Family Law: A more accurate name would probably be "Breaking Up Your Family Law" – but we guess that isn't as catchy. Family lawyers handle all your basic grisly matters outside of criminal court – divorces, child custody battles, child support cases, restraining orders, kidnapping cases, and other lawsuits we all hope will never come our way.

Here's a rule for you, as a prospective consumer of fine legal services: Don't assume *anything* (we all know the joke, right?). If you aren't sure, just *ask*. If you have any concerns at all about whether your lawyer is qualified to do the work you need done, just ask.

Savvy Client Tip: Be sure to interview at least three lawyers before committing to one. Think of the interview as an audition. Even if Contestant #1 is qualified to handle your case, Contestant #2 may be a better fit.

CHAPTER 6

What Kind of Law Firms Are There?

Now you've been primed on the different flavors of lawyers. But practice area isn't the only variable in the "who do I hire" game. What *kind* of practice or firm is also a major variable.

Just as some people love browsing through the gleaming floors of Bloomingdales while others prefer the intimacy of a local mom and pop shop, you may be more comfortable with some kinds of law firms than with others. Good legal services are available at all kinds of firms – just go with the one you like best.

And the cast of characters is ...

Big Firm

Get an idea in your head about what you think a big law firm is. That's probably still not as big as we're talking about here. In the land of the law, "Big Firm" means at least 400 lawyers, several offices worldwide, and with clients like Spain or "Big

Tobacco." We're talking *huge*. The pricing is likewise super-sized at these firms.

Most individuals and small business owners aren't dealing with multimillion-dollar mergers or transactions that have international repercussions. Therefore, you are unlikely to be a good match for a Big Firm, whose strength is in just such matters. But, occasionally you may find that The Guy Who is The Best in a particular niche field works at a Big Firm and he specializes in exactly what you need. If that's the case, and you can afford him, go for it!

Mid-sized Firm

Remember when you were thinking about what a "Big Firm" was? What you had in mind is actually a Mid-sized Firm. In another feat of imprecise language, the term "Mid-sized Firm" applies to anything from 15 lawyers to about 300 lawyers. These firms come in many shapes and sizes, and they handle lots of different kinds of clients with lots of different-sized pocketbooks.

Mid-sized Firms don't have the depth and breadth of the hugest Big Firms, but they are usually well-equipped to handle the most common matters: tax, securities law, corporate law, contracts, etc. Many have multiple offices and are accessible if you live in a large metropolitan area. As a small business owner, developing a relationship with a Mid-sized Firm can be a shrewd move, because it can serve as a one-stop shop for your legal needs. For example, if you have Middleton, Middlebury and Middleschmertz on retainer, you can use Transactional Tara to draft your employment contract one month, and then use Settlement Shamus to handle your divorce the next.

Small Firm

Here, "small" will usually refer both to the size of the office and the size of the staff. We're talking about 2-10 people here. Small doesn't necessarily mean "cheap" when it comes to law firms, but it's a good bet that the rates of a Small Firm are at least a little less than their fancy-pants big-firm counterparts.

Because they're smaller, Small Firms are sometimes limited in the matters they handle. For general legal issues (basic business contracts, estate matters, etc.), Small Firms can be quite sufficient. Good ones also know the other practitioners around town and will refer you if a particular matter seems outside their expertise. One major advantage of dealing with a Small Firm is that the attorney-client relationship can easily become as special as the hairdresser-hairdressee relationship. Your lawyer will learn about you, your family, your business, and your goals – and with that knowledge, will become a valuable member of your personal team.

Solo Practitioner

This is your one-man show. Picture one lone attorney, hanging out a shingle and hoping to one day grow into a Mid-sized Firm. He's doing his own advertising, filing his own papers, answering his own phone calls. He's the everyman of lawyers. Most solo practitioners' rates are relatively low, but the price tag doesn't necessarily indicate anything about his performance. Some sole-practitioners are newbies, while others are seasoned professionals.

If you are working with a solo-practitioner, you need to make sure he or she is competent and experienced with the matter at hand. Beware of anyone (lawyer or not) who claims to be all things to all people. Be direct and ask Solo Solomon: "So, Sol, how many real-estate closings have you done before?" Do research to be sure that your choice is a good one (more on what kind of research in Chapter 8). As long as you choose a solo practitioner whose experience matches your needs, a one-man-show can be a great choice. A lawyer with this kind of firm will work hard to keep every client he gets, and you will likely get first-class service at a reasonable price.

Boutique

"Boutique" means the same thing in law firms that it does in shoe-stores. Small. Specialized. Fancy. Law firms that call themselves "Boutique Firms" are usually 5-30 lawyers, all of whom used to work in Big Firms, who have branched out on their own to handle cases in one particular practice area. We know what you're thinking. Big-firm lawyers for small-firm pricetags? Sort of. Former Big-Firm types often leave their $500-per-hour firms when they realize that they can do the same work for the same clients and charge only $300 per hour. Because the Boutique Firm has much lower overhead than Monolith & Monolith, PC, more cash goes in Boutique Bob's pockets, and your bill is lowered. It's a win-win that only a lawyer could dream up.

Choosing to work with a Boutique Law Firm is usually dictated by the matter at hand or an existing relationship with an attorney who transferred from another firm. If you have a specialized matter that falls within the firm's specialty, you can be sure that you'll get cutting-edge legal knowledge and excellent service at a Boutique.

Savvy Client Tip:

Have a clear image of what kind of lawyer you'd like to hire, and then seek out a perfect match.

CHAPTER 7

Figuring Out What Kind of Lawyer You Want

You're ready to write the check, you know what *kind* of lawyer you need, and from what sort of firm, but you're not exactly sure *who* is your perfect legal match. Should you hire Snarkle McSnarkleson, whose ad you saw on the side of a bus? Or should you hire Patti Passivinsky, who is your college roommate's sister? You can't exactly put an ad in the personals that says "Needy Client with great credit seeks ethical, assertive, legal representation with low price tag."

So what *can* you do?

We hate to get all new-agey on you, but the first step is to look *inward*. *Why* are you hiring this lawyer? *What role* will he or she play in your life? *What results* are you trying to achieve? The smart client asks these questions first, to ensure that when he hires a law firm, it's a match made in legal heaven.

Lawyers can potentially serve two roles: the role of an **advisor** or the role of a **representative.**

If you're hiring a lawyer as an **advisor**, think about your own learning style. Are you most comfortable learning information from a buddy, who will pick up the phone on the first ring and answer your question in ten words or less? Or are you more comfortable in a formal setting as a professor-like figure leads you through your query in intricate detail? The most important thing to do when hiring an advisor-type lawyer is to create a relationship that you will be **comfortable using and likely to maintain**. There's no right answer here . . . it's all about personal preference.

If you're hiring a lawyer as your **representative**, then you should think about whom you'd cast in role of *you* in this particular legal drama. Your lawyer will be speaking on your behalf and in your place. In some matters, you may prefer an ultra-aggressive, fear-inspiring shark. In others, you may prefer a friendly plays-well-with-others mediator. Think about what you need to achieve and who you'd like to be. Then seek out a lawyer who will be your best courtroom avatar.

When Elura worked as a prosecutor, she often found herself pitted against a defense lawyer who was intimidating if not outright scary. A former NYPD officer, and oversized Fred Flintstone-look alike, this guy could take control of any courtroom. And if his size wasn't enough, he *really* knew his stuff, and regularly bellowed brilliant legal arguments through the courtroom in a booming baritone. This was the kind of guy that – law degree or no law degree – we all hoped *never* to get into an argument with. We never invite him to dinner parties or golf outings, and if we do see him in social situations, we still shudder a bit. In short, he's one of our *favorite* lawyers and we refer a lot of business to him. Get the picture?

If your lawyer-to-be will be both your advisor and your representative, be sure to picture her in both roles before making your final decision. A dual-action lawyer should be both easy to work with and also a great advocate for your interests.

Often, finding the perfect attorney-client match to your needs can make a tremendous difference in your ultimate outcome. Once you've found a couple of names that seem like good contenders, remember that you can always interview or even audition several different lawyers until you find one with whom you'd like to do business. Don't feel guilty! You're about to pay someone a lot of money to do something that is very important.

Savvy Client Tip: **Get to high ground before the waves hit. In other words, develop relationships with several lawyers BEFORE you really need one.**

Once you've determined who your dream lawyer would be, how do you find him or her? How do you tell whether the lawyer you are considering is Sharon the Shark or Sharon the Sheep? How do you even find the name of someone to call?

CHAPTER 8

Finding the Perfect Attorney-Client Match

F inding a lawyer is a lot like buying a mattress. It's going to take some time. It's not going to be particularly fun. Comparison-shopping is very complicated. But when you find the right one, you'll sleep better all night. The dustier our diplomas get, the more ridiculous some "How I Found My Lawyer" stories become. We've heard them all, from "His office is on my way home from work," to "He seemed like a real jerk so I figured he'd be a *great* lawyer." People who are usually smart and otherwise savvy often check their common sense at the door when hiring a lawyer. This is not the time to be passive. By asking a few pointed questions, you can find out quite a lot about your potential new advocate.

Make sure you clarify with the attorney up-front that he will not be charging you for the initial interview. Most lawyers don't charge for an initial consultation. But don't assume anything. Clarify that because you are not asking for immediate

HERE ARE SOME OF THE WAYS YOU CAN RESEARCH LAWYERS

Lists

- ✓ Paid Legal Referral services
- ✓ Online directories
- ✓ State Bar Association membership rosters
- ✓ The Yellow Pages
- ✓ Other alphabetical piles of information

Pros	Con
It's easy. Lists may help you find someone in a unique practice area (like a "rare-coin collectible litigator") or targeted demographic (like "Christian Women Attorneys").	Other than the person's name, address, phone number, and practice area, you're not going to get much more information out of a list. If the list you're using only has a few lawyers on it, you may want to start here and then conduct a personal interview with your candidates.

Internet

Pro	Con
It's got everything. The only way to really use the internet as a great lawyer-search tool is to see what people are saying about the work a lawyer has done. Blogs, press write-ups, and other accounts of first-hand dealings with a lawyer or law firm can be great tools in narrowing your search.	It's got everything. Including an abundance of unhelpful information. Lawyers (as well as others) can be held hostage by a single bad review posted by someone with an axe to grind. As an innocent Googler, you won't be sure whether to trust the five-diamond rating on one website, or the triple-thumbs-down on another.

HERE ARE SOME OF THE WAYS YOU CAN RESEARCH LAWYERS

Referrals from friends

Pro	Con
You can ask questions about why your friend liked working with that particular lawyer, and you can get honest, inside information about the lawyer's style and work ethic.	This is a limited resource. Using your friend's lawyer can present the same concerns as using your friend's hairdresser. What she loves, you may hate, and what you need may be very different than what she needed.

legal advice that you won't have to pay. And if you feel awkward clarifying that point so early in your burgeoning relationship . . . get over it. You're going to spend hundreds and possibly thousands of dollars hiring a lawyer. The sooner you take control, the better.

Here are some examples of questions you could ask during your search for the perfect lawyer:

✓ How many _____ (insert name of legal document to be drafted) have you done?

✓ How long have you been doing this?

✓ What would you say your litigation style is?

✓ Have you ever handled a case that is just like mine?

✓ What do your clients say is best about your representation?

✓ Do you have any other trials or cases coming up that might interfere in any way with my case?

✓ Why should I hire you?

Here's a handy-dandy worksheet that you can use to help guide you through your first meeting with your potential lawyer-to-be.

Attorney Questionaire

Today's Date: _____

Attorney Name: _____

Address: _____Email:_____

Telephone number: _____Fax: _____

Years in Practice: _____

Experience handling cases like mine:

_____

_____

Fee Structure: _____

_____

Questions I'm planning to ask today:

- What is your plan for handling this matter? I'd like a step-by-step description please.
- Is there anything that makes my case different or more complicated?
- What is your preferred method of communication?
- How often can I expect to reach you when I call?
- Will you be handling the bulk of the work? If not you, who?

_____

_____

_____

Notes:

_____

_____

_____

_____

_____

Take notes. No one can remember everything.

Once you've found the perfect firm to handle your legal needs, it's important to have a clear understanding about *who* is actually doing *what* on your legal matter. Some matters require an entire legal team of professionals, including associates, partners, paralegals, clerks, and other support staff. Other matters will be handled by an associate who you may never meet, and will be simply supervised by the partner who calls you with updates. You need to be involved with these choices, because you'll be paying for everyone's time, and you'll be paying higher hourly rates as you move up the law-firm food chain.

As the consumer of legal services, you need to know that you can take control here. Many clients think of law firms the way they think of sports cars. They pay no attention to the inner workings, and they never dream of fiddling with or adjusting anything. They just get in and go for a ride . . . and complain about the astronomical cost of repairs. With a law firm, you *can* and *should* adjust things to your liking. You may prefer that only partners work on your case, because they are more efficient and experienced. You may prefer that one specific senior associate handle all your matters because you like him best. There is no one right thing to request – the point here is that you should learn about your choices and ask for what you want.

If you are in the kind of business where you're definitely going to need a lawyer sometime in the future, it's a good idea to start looking for one *now*. People make the best decisions when the pressure is off. By researching, interviewing and hiring an attorney before you are desperate for one, you'll make a better decision and be more satisfied with the one you hire.

Often, finding the perfect attorney-client match to your needs can make a tremendous difference in your ultimate outcome. For example, Vito, owned *Meatland,* a neighborhood-renowned pork store in Brooklyn. (For those of you non-New Yorkers, a "pork store" is what we call an "Italian Deli" – a neighborhood shop packed with salty and cheesy goodness and imported specialties guaranteed to bring on a coronary in the next quarter-hour.) Across the block, Vito's arch-nemesis, Filomena, was at the helm of *Pork Supreme, Meatland's* biggest competitor. *Pork Supreme* had been in financial trouble, and Vito was convinced that under his fearless leadership, he could help it rise to greatness under the umbrella of the growing *Meatland* empire, with Vito himself crowned the Pork King of Bensonhurst.

Vito knew his overall goal, but wasn't sure about the details. Was a merger the right thing to propose? A hostile takeover? A buy-out? And even if he knew his legal strategy, how was he going to broach the topic with Filomena? Should he allow her behind his own deli counter to witness his operations without making her sign a confidentiality agreement?

Vito found a lawyer who was familiar with both mergers and mozzarella, and engaged him to advise and represent him in this deal. The lawyer helped draft a Non-Disclosure Agreement, a Memorandum of Understanding that spelled out the general terms of agreement between Vito and Filomena, the final Purchase and Sale Agreement and the new Shareholders' Agreement. The lawyer also recommended a financial advisor who helped Vito come up with a strategy for valuing both businesses and a fair compensation scheme that worked for everyone. The financial

Savvy Client Tip:

The best defense is a good offense.

advisor and the attorney worked together with Vito to discuss all the options and hammer out potential details. During the Vito-Filomena Summit, Vito decided to have his lawyer represent him during the discussion of any sensitive issues. The result? *Porkland Supreme* is now a thriving business, and Vito and Filomena are happily married and planning to start their own sausage-loving family. By hiring a lawyer who truly understood his unique business and the legal ramifications of various changes, Vito ensured that negotiations and decisions were made in the most effective way possible.

> **Savvy Client Tip:** **Interview potential attorneys over the phone, and keep your list of questions in front of you as you speak with each "contestant."**

OK, this tip is for those of you who eat "savvy" for breakfast. In litigation, strategy wins the game . . . and with this little trick, you can put your strategy into place before any lawsuit is even *filed*. How? Establish working relationships with more than one law firm. If you already work with the top three law firms in town, none of those firms will be permitted to represent any opponent of yours in any case because of conflict-of-interest rules. If you end up in litigation, you'll have outmaneuvered your opponent before the first court date. While you're working on preparing for court, the other party will be frantically shopping around for lawyers!

CHAPTER 9

Paying Your Lawyer

Before we give you any specific advice about keeping your legal bills manageable, we need to remind you to check on the status of your backbone. Whether you receive a bill for $500 or $5,000 or $50,000, you must pay attention and take control. If you've been billed for something that you think is unfair, then speak up!

Do we think all lawyers are rapacious fee-grabbing bastards? No. We know nearly all lawyers are well-intentioned, hard-working professionals. But they are people, too, subject to mistake and oversight, like the rest of us. And then there is "the system." The business of the practice of law is inherently problematic, and creates opportunities for sloppiness and mis-statements.

Here's some motivational truth for you: back when we were pinstripe-wearing associates working for large law firms, we were privy to all sorts of billing slip-ups (*our* clients, of course, were never the victims). Some were quite egregious. We used to close our office doors and whisper to each other about the inevitable shouting that would result when the clients got their inflated bills. But we were wrong. The clients *never* complained. They were rarely paying attention enough to complain. Perhaps these clients were so wowed by the $5,000 floral arrangements in the lobby and so intimidated by the lead partner's blustering demeanor that they paid their bills without asking a single question.

But since you're reading this book, we assume that you're not one of *those* clients. *You* would like to be the kind of client who saddles up and wrangles any out-of-control lawyer in your path, right? Channel your favorite straight-shooter, and if you feel like the partner handling your case is a certified ambassador of baloney, then step in and speak up.

And there are plenty of things you can do to stretch your legal dollars even without complaining. Negotiating the right fee structure and billing format at the start of your relationship is key. We know – when it comes to hiring a professional, you hate to negotiate. It just feels *icky*. Most of us prefer to save our haggling maneuvers for car salesmen or real-estate agents. But remember – your money is yours to protect. Your business is *valuable*.

Savvy Client Tip: Any time you're having a document drafted, check around with friends and colleagues to see if they need similar documents drafted. Maybe you can request a bulk discount from your lawyer.

Another little inside secret: law firms have some of the best facades in the world. Really. The ability of some firms to create an illusion sometimes rivals that of Disney. Part of the business of practicing law requires lawyers to exaggerate the size of their firms and their number of clients. After all, a lawyer who announced at a real-estate closing that this was her very first deal, and that her office is in her two-room apartment might open herself up to some trouble at the counsel table. But don't allow yourself to be bamboozled out of knowing the value of your business. Know that regardless of the size of your firm or the size of your business, they *want* you to stay. And if it's a lousy economy or your lawyer is branching out into new practice areas, it's very likely that he'd be willing to budge on his prices. So just *ask*.

Now that you've got the lasso and the whip, it's time to dig in and learn about how the money part of lawyer-client relationships can work. Different kinds of legal work go hand in hand with different kinds of fee arrangements. By learning the ins and outs of each fee arrangement, you can create a more productive relationship with your attorney and stretch your legal dollars farther.

Communication with your attorney remains key no matter what kind of fee structure you are using. Learn the options available to you, negotiate as much as you can, and don't agree to anything that seems not-quite-right to you.

Savvy Client Tip:

Offering your lawyer some great press may be a great way to cut down your bill if he's trying to expand his practice.

Savvy Client Tip: Find out who will actually be doing the bulk of the work on your case.

CHAPTER 10

Legal Fee Structures: Variations on a Theme

Different kinds of legal work go hand in hand with different kinds of fee arrangements. By learning the ins and outs of each fee arrangement, you can create a more productive relationship with your attorney and stretch your legal dollars farther. Traditionally, there were three kinds of fee structures: Contingency-Fee Agreements, Flat-Fee Agreements, and Hourly Retainers. Each of those has high points and low points that we'll discuss below. These days, clients are smarter than ever, and as a result, the traditional fee arrangements have evolved into some cooler and less-scary options.

Traditional Fee Structures

Contingency Fee Agreements

Applications: Personal injury or other tort cases, or anything where you might "win" money in a verdict or settlement. (Note that we're not talking about commercial or contracts disputes here. Those are usually handled hourly, not on contingency.)

The Arrangement: You pay your lawyer *absolutely nothing* to start with. He works on your case, and then *if* you win, he gets a piece of your winnings.

The Hook: You know those lawyers who advertise their services during daytime TV? They're always yapping about the "free consultation." Well, don't get too excited. The "free consultation" is legal equivalent of selling tap water. *Every* lawyer who works on contingencies does the consultation for free. If the lawyer thinks your case is a winner, he'll spend the time trying to hook you as a client. If he thinks your case is a loser, he'll probably have his secretary fake an emergency and usher you out the door faster than you can say "retainer."

The Poison: Contingency fee agreements can be enticing and practical, because you don't need to go into your own pocket to pay your legal bills. But many clients are surprised by the end result of their contingency fee agreement because of the "costs" aspect.

The Antidote:
- ✓ Learn what costs will be passed along to you, and be clear that you refuse to pay for anything to which you haven't specifically agreed.
- ✓ Negotiate to have the lawyer bear some of the costs. Be reasonable, though. Asking your lawyer to bear the cost of a few hundred copies is reasonable when the firm stands

to make $100,000 on a settlement. Asking your lawyer to pay a $25,000 expert witness fee is too much.

✓ Negotiate the percentage to which your lawyer will be entitled. You may prefer to allow your lawyer a higher percentage as his fee for services, but with costs *included*. You might prefer a sliding-scale recovery system, in which your attorney takes a larger percentage as your overall recovery increases. If your case is a strong one, your lawyer will likely be willing to negotiate to some degree.

✓ Offer exposure to your lawyer. Many tort cases have juicy details that the local press would love to hear. Maybe you can offer to include your lawyer's name in a press release or mass e-mail to your contacts. Many lawyers would be willing to adjust their prices for such solid publicity. Just be sure to discuss the details of this kind of arrangement with your lawyer before talking with the media, because some settlements will require that you keep the details confidential.

Here's how it really works: Your contingency-fee agreement might entitle your lawyer to 30% of your recovery *after costs*. So let's say that you are suing the circus after being trampled by their famous troupe of tap-dancing elephants. Your lawyer may have traveled to Timbuktu to interview expert elephan-tologists, which cost him $40,000. Even if you won your case and got $100,000 in damages, the first $40,000 comes off the top to pay for the "costs." Then, your lawyer is entitled to 30% of the remaining $60,000, and you get the rest. It's only fair that the attorney be reimbursed for these costs, but keep a tight leash on it, and make sure that he hires a reasonably-priced elephantologist.

Flat Fee Arrangements

Applications: Document drafting, estate-planning, business incorporation, simple divorces, low-level criminal or municipal matters, certain intellectual property filings, and some transactional work.

The Arrangement: You pay your lawyer a fixed price to handle a specific matter, and that's the end of it.

The Hook: Flat fees can be great, because they have the lowest risk of snowballing.

The Poison: How does your lawyer make money on "flat fee" cases? Simple. He charges $500 to handle your case, and then ignores you as much as possible. If he's *really* organized, he'll delegate your entire matter to his paralegal, and never talk to you again until the whole thing is finished. As long as your matter is being properly supervised, there's not necessarily anything wrong with this kind of system. However, the most common complaint that people have with their lawyers is that the lawyer doesn't call back. Want to be sure that your lawyer calls you back promptly? Pay him by the hour to do so. The Flat-Fee Arrangement presupposes that you want your matter handled, but that you don't need much hand-holding. Think about your needs realistically. Are you likely to call your lawyer every week? If so, you may be much more satisfied with a different kind of arrangement.

The Antidote:
- ✓ Bartering or referring other clients
- ✓ Remember – your lawyer is running a business too! Do you have connections to goods or services that your lawyer might desperately need? Your lawyer might be thrilled to barter with you. Maybe you can trade your interior decorating services for an employment agreement. Maybe you can fix his copy machine while he fixes your

will. Even better, maybe you can get a package deal if he handles your will and your next-door neighbor's will.

Bartering will probably work better with a solo practitioner than a larger firm, and is more likely to be successful with an attorney with whom you've already maintained a successful business relationship.

Just be reasonable and don't try to pay for your real-estate closing in chickens.

Hourly Fees Deducted From a Retainer

In this case, your attorney will charge you an up-front fee which you will pay before work on your behalf begins. As your case proceeds, the charges will be set against the retainer until it is used up. If you end up racking up more fees than were initially provided, you will have to pony up more money. If you don't, the excess retainer fees should be returned to you.

Applications: Defense of any lawsuit, general advising, complex matters of any kind, many transactions, non-contingency lawsuits, and anything that doesn't fall within the other categories.

The Arrangement: Simple, yet terrifying. You pay a specified hourly-rate for each individual who works on your case. Hourly rates vary a lot, depending on where (geographically) you are, what kind of matter you are pursuing, the amount of money that's at stake, and the seniority of the lawyer. Everyone knows that things cost more money in big cities. That rule is no different whether you're hiring a lawyer or booking a hotel room. For example, a New York City senior partner may bill out at up to $1,000 an hour (eek!), but equally-competent senior partners in central Pennsylvania might be only about one-third of that cost. As a very general rule, you'll probably have to pay $175-250 for junior lawyers or solo-practitioners, $250-400 for senior lawyers or low-level big-shots, and $400-700 for super fancy-pants partners. Paralegals also get in on the fees, usually billing between $100 and $200 an hour depending on their experience.

The Hook: In theory, this works like a calling-card – you pay only for exactly what you use.

The Poison: This is the most common and most terrifying of fee arrangements. This is why there are lawyer jokes. It's a potential monetary black hole and everyone knows it. The hourly rate will be high, and you'll be billed in six-minute increments, always rounded *up*. That means that if your $225-an-hour lawyer calls you and leaves you a thirty-second voice-mail, you'll get a bill for $37. 50 before you even call him back.

Savvy Client Tip: **Make sure your retainer agreement specifically says that any unused portion of your retainer funds will be promptly returned to you.**

Hourly fees have the overwhelming tendency to snowball, for a variety of reasons. As with any other profession, there are lawyers out there who are dishonest – but fee snowballing can be a problem even when your lawyer is being completely honest and ethical.

Some of the most common causes of fee-snowballing are:
- Billing for time spent reading up on or learning an entirely new practice area. This is work that must be done, but you may not want to have your lawyer learn on your dime.
- Billing for time spent "thinking" or "strategizing" about a case, even when that thinking occurred while driving home, taking a shower, or working on another case.

- "Double billing" two clients equally for work that was only done one time, but benefitted both of them.

- Billing for time spent negotiating the details of a transaction that could easily have been negotiated directly between you and the other party.

- Billing for time spent repeating explanations or instructions to you, because you were not adequately prepared for your part in a lawsuit.

The Antidote:

✓ Pay attention. Complain. Negotiate.

✓ Stop treating your lawyer like he's The-Great-and-Powerful Oz. Pull back the curtain, learn what's going on inside the firm, and take control, just as you would with your hairdresser, your landscaper, or your housekeeper. Set up parameters for what you will and will not pay, and make sure that you look closely at your monthly statement.

✓ Use common sense. If your statement lists seventeen hours of legal research for your lawyer to draft a two-page document, ask why it took so long. Sure, it's possible that the project was more complex than it seems on the surface. But don't assume. Show your lawyer that you're monitoring his performance. The closer you scrutinize your bill, the more responsible your lawyer will be with his billing. It's just human nature.

We are certainly not suggesting that lawyers are all sitting around, greedily milking their clients while lining their own pocket.

CREATIVE FEE STRUCTURES

Now that you have a good handle on *traditional* fee structures, we've got some incredible news: these days, even in the legal world, where the concept of "dress-down-Fridays" is considered sacrilegious, lawyers are becoming more flexible with billing structures. Law firms may never stop being ensconced in pinstripes and mahogany, but some are willing to be forward thinking when it comes to money. Here are some of the more creative ways lawyers and law firms have devised to separate you from your money. If any of them appeal to you, be sure to suggest them the next time you hire a law firm.

Blended rates

Picture it: your case will be handled by Senior Partner Patrick McPartnerson XVII, whose great-great-grandfather founded the law firm, and whose time is billed at $500 per hour, *and* by Lowell Lowman, a junior associate who bills out at only $300 per hour (sorry, we had to say "only" there). You might agree to a "blended rate" of $400 per hour for all time spent on your case, regardless of which lawyer is actually doing the work. Blended rates can be a great way of creating the right work-supervision-fee balance for your case. Just be sure that before you agree on a blended rate, that you are comfortable the level of supervision that the senior lawyer will be giving to your case.

Capped Fees

Clients who hear about "capped fees" might think, "Sweet Mama! My prayers have been answered!" A firm that has handled matters just like yours a zillion times before might be willing to charge you hourly, but to cap it at some defined maximum. Because the firm can predict approximately how much work your matter will require, it may be willing to commit to a maximum fee, which is great for you, because it allows you to budget. It can be very liberating to say, "I'll pay $300 an hour, but I won't pay a penny over $6,000." However, (and you knew this was coming) there is likely to be a safety net built into the firm's capped fee structure. So if your child-custody battle suddenly spins out of control and dominoes into multinational commercial litigation, you'll probably have to pay extra.

Success Fee

Sometimes, clients feel the urge to tip their attorney for a job well done (usually, clients do this by mounting a unicorn, flying by their attorney's office on a rainbow, clutching the pot of gold handed to them by a magical dwarf, eager to hand it over to the senior partner of Arye, Ewe, Kidd & Mei). More often, clients feel that when there is a less than favorable result, they should be entitled to a discount. A Success Fee arrangement would mean that if your lawyer wins the case on your behalf, you'll pay extra, but if your team loses, you'll get a discount. The same idea can also be used with deadlines. For example, if your deal closes by January 1, you agree to pay the lawyers 125% of the fees they've earned, but if it closes after March 1, you only have to pay 80% of the fees. Using a Success Fee can be risky for both the lawyer and the client – but if it works for your matter, it may help both sides walk away happier than ever.

Under-Budget Incentives

This is where your lawyer estimates a total fee for the work about to be done on your case. Then, you agree that if the lawyer completes the matter completes the matter at a lower cost than estimated, that you'll pay the firm some kind of bonus.

Reduced Hourly Rates and Contingency

This is a combination of an hourly rate and a contingency fee arrangement. Let's say you've been sued when Litigious Lititia fell in your store. You've agreed to pay your lawyer an hourly fee for the defense, and you've accepted that you'll probably have to pay Lititia about $100,000 to settle the case. If your lawyer is able to settle the case for only $25,000, then the firm would be entitled to some percentage of the $75,000 that they "saved" you.

Reverse Contingency Fee

Picture it: you owe $200,000 in back taxes to the IRS. You hire a law firm to help you deal with the giant mess, and somehow, your lawyer settles the whole matter for only $150,000. A reverse contingency fee arrangement would mean that the amount you'd pay the firm is some percentage of the $50,000 that their work just "saved" you.

Dedicated or "Rented" Lawyer

You own a business, and what you really need is your own in-house counsel. But you don't have one. Maybe you'd decide to "rent" a lawyer from the firm of Weegotem & Howe by paying a fixed amount to have a lawyer be completely dedicated to your needs for a fixed amount of time.

Piece of the Action

Picture it: you have a startup company that you know is just about to hit it big. You may find a lawyer or firm that is willing to accept profit-sharing in your company as compensation for legal work. This could be a great way to do what is essentially large-scale bartering, or could be very risky if the firm ends up caring more about your profits than about solid legal advice.

Prepaid Legal Services

Some firms (or some groups of firms working together) offer plans where, for a specified monthly or annual fee, you are entitled to a bundle of legal services. For example, you may pay $10,000 for the year and get 30 hours of telephone consultation, 5 hours of contract review, 5 miscellaneous hours, drafting of a will, a power of attorney and a healthcare proxy. Firms love these arrangements just like health clubs do: many people buy the services and then never use them. But a savvy client like you could use this really wisely. For example, if you've already pre-paid, you could use some of your consultation hours to learn about ways to avoid lawsuits. You could even use the time to have your top managers consult directly with lawyers to learn what they can do to minimize exposure to risk.

Group Legal Services

If health insurance and law firms had a love-child, it would be Group Legal Services. You get together with a big group of other people, and pay a relatively low premium. Then, when one member of your group needs a lawyer, you're entitled to use your group's law firm for consultation or representation.

Savvy Client Tip: Be clear about things for which you refuse to pay. If you are clear and firm from the start, there's less of a chance for fees to snowball.

CHAPTER 11

De-Mystifying Your Legal Bill

The fee structure you've agreed upon with your attorney is really only part of the total fees-for-services equation. To avoid feeling blindsided after receiving your bill, you also need to have the right relationship with the bill itself. The format of the bill should be clear and easy to understand; a monthly invoice is a tool for *you*, not some inside-the-law-firm document that is written in an alien code. If you don't get what the entries on your statement mean, speak up. By ensuring that you know the exact work that is being performed, exactly who is doing that work, and exactly what you are paying for that work, you can limit surprises and be comfortable paying your bill.

The right lawyer, the right fee arrangement and the right billing format are all pieces of the Using Legal Dollars Wisely puzzle. But the most important piece is your own vigilance.

Pay attention to the work that's being done and use the power of negotiation as much as you can. And you must scrutinize your bill with all the focus and skepticism you can rally. We know a great many lawyers who work very hard, have buckets of integrity, and even *underbill* their clients (yes, if you call us, we'll give you their numbers!). The point is that the legal industry itself is quite varied when it comes to billing practices, and many lawyers are negotiable about certain fees. It can't hurt to ask politely.

Whether you are a big or small client, it's perfectly reasonable for you to request that you:

- Will not pay for meals or ordinary travel costs.
- Wish to have a $200-per-hour associate handle your entire matter, rather than a $600-per-hour partner.
- Expect not to be billed for time spent waiting, relaxing, or brainstorming.
- Will pay a reduced rate for copies, phone calls, and faxes.
- Are only corresponded with via e-mail, so as to save mailing costs.
- Get a full explanation of each entry on your statement.

If you are not a seasoned complainer, now is a good time to start learning. So long as you pay your bills in a timely way, you have every right to complain when you feel that you've been overbilled. Remember the old saying: "A drip makes a puddle." You may only be able to cut down your legal bills $50 at a time. But every bit helps. Plus, sharpening your skills as a savvy client will help you learn how to effectively wrangle your lawyer in the future – and will remind your lawyer that no matter how fancy her office may be, *you* are still her boss.

And let us just take a minute to say that we know that what we are suggesting you do isn't necessarily easy. Many of us pride ourselves on our ability to work well with others while being positive and optimistic. And for some of us, personally, emotionally, or culturally, complaining isn't easy. And when the object of your grievance is a Jaguar-driving, fast-talking courtroom bulldog, mustering up the confidence to voice an objection is easier said than done. But you can find your own effective style of complaining that is comfortable for you.

Recently, we found ourselves in the uncomfortable position of being complaining clients. Based on a friend's referral, we'd hired a well-known boutique law firm to draft a complex contract for us. Unfortunately, before the contract was finalized, the lawyer handling it left the firm and instructed his colleagues to finish the contract and e-mail it to us. While the completed contract never found its way to us, the bill for services certainly did – by e-mail, snail mail, and telephone call. We were tempted to march into the firm's lobby and announce our formation of a new Facebook group called "This Guy's Firm Sucks," but decided to take a sweeter approach. We sent an e-mail to the managing partner of the firm explaining that we know how employee turnover can sometimes throw a wrench into any business, but that we have the utmost faith that his firm would do the right thing. And they did. No questions asked, and no uncomfortable argument required.

Don't feel that you have to have the debating powers of Lincoln or Douglas to effectively raise a complaint. Do it in *your* voice, and in *your* style. If you're honest, direct, and clear, you'll get good results.

Savvy Client Tip: During your initial interview with your lawyer, ask to see a sample billing statement.

The Law Firm of William Billings Billingsly
The Billings Building

Most firms use "client-matter numbers" in which the first number identifies the client and the second number identifies the particular matter being handled. Here, the client-matter number ends in 00004, indicating that this is the fourth legal matter handled by this firm for this client.

October 19, 2012

Clotilda Client
202 1st Street
Novato CA 94009

This is the identification number that the court is using to identify your case.

Invoice number: 225

You're paying both lawyers hourly so that they can discuss your matter together. Consider asking for a blended rate so that you're not being milked for their cooperation. 1.1 hours for lunch seems reasonable. But did you get hit with the lunch bill too? Makes sure that the firm didn't use this meeting as an excuse to rack up $400 in escargot costs.

Client-Matter number: 12450-00004
Docket (case) number: CM-12056/12

Statement of Services Rendered

Date	Atty	Services rendered	Hours	Amount
09/24/12	PSP&ASA	Lunch meeting with Isabella and Ferdinand to discuss recent proposal from Chris (1.1)	1.1	$ 770.00
09/25/12	PSP	Telephone conference maritime law (3 All this editing and discussing may seem redundant when listed this way, but it probably isn't.		
09/26/12	ASA	Preparation of Articles of Dissolution per client's request (.7); Edited Articles of Dissolution (.3); Discussed edits with PSP. Review of edited Articles of Dissolution (.5); Discussed edits with PSP (.5)	2.0	$ 600.00
09/26/12	PSP	Lawyers sometimes like to "round up" time spent on phone calls. Make sure your own records match your bill. A few minutes on each side of a phone call for preparation is reasonable, but an extra half-hour is not.		
09/26/12	PSP	Telephone conference with opposing counsel regarding settlement (2.5)	2.5	$1,000.00
09/28/12	LEL	Research regarding res ipsa Loquitor (.8)	.8	$ 160.00
09/29/12	LEL	Prepared final draft of Articles of Dissolution (.8)	.8	$ 160.00
09/30/12	ASP	Attended motion conference in Superior Court per client's request (5.0); Edited Articles of Dissolution (.3); Discussed edits with PSP. Review of edited Articles of Dissolution (.5); Discussed edits with PSP (.5)	6.3	$1,890.00

Total professional services rendered through 09/30/12   17.4 $6,140.00

We know you hate paying for research, but it's important and necessary. However, there's a difference between researching a groundbreaking precedent that directly impacts your case and reading the law journal for fun. Be sure to ask about the purpose and outcome of any legal research. You'll keep the firm on a tight leash.

Be sure you've seen the document you purchased.

Page 1 of 2

An hour is a long time for anything other than a trial. Lawyers often bill for waiting time in court. Speak up and make sure you're clear about how your retainer is being used.

The Law Firm of William Billings Billingsly
The Billings Building
100 Broadway
New York, NY 10010

October 19, 2012
Clotilda Client
Invoice number:

Are you being billed for overnight delivery of mail when you could have dropped by your attorney's office on your way home from work? If so, call his secretary and request that she call you before sending any documents out

Client-Matter number: 1 60-00004
Docket (case) number: .-12056/12

Statement of Services Rendered, continued

Summary	Hours	Rate	Amount
Paul S. Partnerson	7.5	400.00	3,000.00
Abel S. Associate	8.3	300.00	2,490.00
Lowell E. Associate	1.6	200.00	320.00

Costs advanced	Amount
09/26/12 Photocopy charge	0.67
09/26/12 Postage	0.30
09/30/12 Messenger Service	27.00
Total advanced costs	$27.41

Total current fees and costs $ 5,937.41

Prior balance $16,977.40

Retainer applied   ($600.00)

Total amount due and payable $22,214.81

===============

Previous retainer account balance $5,000.00
09/15/12 Transfer from retainer account to reimburse firm for
          professional services and advanced costs   600.00-

                                 Net change to retainer account $600.00-
                                                                  ----
                        Remaining retainer balance on 09/30/12 $4,400.00
                                                                  ===========

* Is there a cost that you don't understand? Speak up! It's probably legit, but you'd check if it were your Visa bill!

Page 2 of 2

The Law Firm of Dirk Notsacheap
The Firm Building
100 Broadway
New York, NY 10010

October 19, 2012

Here is the client and matter number that we saw earlier.

Justina Minute
202 1st Street
Novato CA 94009

Invoice number: 225

Client-Matter number: 246-005687
Docket (case) number: DN-56101/12

This bill categorizes the work with subheadings and then itemizes the corresponding work performed.

Date	Atty	Services Rendered	Hours	Amount

Case Assessment, Development and Administration

| 02/05/07 | PSP | Meeting with expert, B. Schwartz in his Santa Monica, CA office | 1.5 | $412.50 |

Drafting of documents

| 2/14/07 | PSP | Draft report of meeting with B. Schwartz | 0.8 | $220.00 |

Discovery - L300

Hey! Did you just get charged for a deposition that was a no-show? Ask your attorney to adjust his rate for waiting around.

| 02/12/07 | JSLR | Appear for no-show deposition of witness | 2.5 | $900.00 |
| 02/21/07 | JSLR | Expert discovery of B. Schwartz | 0.2 | $ 72.00 |

Trial Preparation and Trial - L400

02/11/07	LL	Conference with opp atty re: sched of next conf	2.5	$312.50
02/18/07	PHR	Scheduling of trial setting conference	0.3	$ 60.00
02/21/07	LL	Trial setting conference	0.4	$ 50.00

Balance from last bill: $1,375.00
Balance from current bill: $2,027.00

Total: $3,402.00

Two and a half hours to schedule a conference?

Savvy Client Tip:

If you are going to get rid of your attorney, do it sooner because you will be hurting yourself if you try to do it later. It will grind your matter to a halt. That's bound to annoy you. And what's worse is that if your matter is being litigated, the court probably won't give you any extra time for your new lawyer to get up to speed. That's both annoying and dangerous.

CHAPTER 12

Setting Up the Right Balance of Power

You don't want to find yourself in a situation where you feel like your attorney is in charge. Feeling like you answer to your lawyer will limit your ability to effectively communicate with him, and that's not good. Sure, most people agree conceptually that their lawyer works for them ... but there's just *something* about the attorney-client relationship that makes clients feel as if they are answering to their own lawyers.

If you've hired a lawyer, it's because you're in a jam, because you're vulnerable, or because the lawyer knows things that you don't know. And the attorney is the one who is directly in the line of fire. *She* talks to the judge, *she's* at the closing, and *she* does the negotiating. You hired her to steer the ship of your case, and as a result, you can end up feeling like she's, well ... *in charge*.

The attorney-client relationship can all go wrong if the client (you) feels intimidated. When clients feel inferior to their hired counsel, it can create a wag-the-dog situation. Plus, you're paying the bill . . . shouldn't you feel *good*?

Savvy Client Tip: E-mailing a meeting agenda to your lawyer before your conference is a great way to take control over the attorney-client relationship.

HERE ARE SOME TIPS TO HELP MAINTAIN THE RIGHT BALANCE OF POWER

Remember that you're no dummy. There are things that you don't know and that's okay.

You hired a lawyer because he knows how do something that you don't know how to do. It's silly to feel inadequate or inferior because he has specialized knowledge that you don't have. We're now giving you permission not to know everything. Okay? There. Now you can be a better client. By giving up the insecurity, you can focus on what's really important – getting your attorney to do your legal work the way you want it done. When you hire a jeweler, a landscaper, a hairdresser, or a plumber, does their specialized knowledge make you feel inadequate? Probably not. Think of your lawyer in the same way. Get comfortable saying "I don't understand," and "Can you explain that?" because it is critical that you understand what your lawyer is talking about! You're already on your attorney's good side because you're paying the bill; you don't also have to impress him with your dazzling intellect.

Embrace your role as a consumer.

Understanding your role in the attorney-client relationship is the key to maximizing the effectiveness of that relationship. In restaurants and department stores, patrons usually have no trouble embracing their roles as consumers. When you eat at La Snotty Restaurant Du Jour, it's understood that the staff needs to please you with its cuisine and service. When you shop at Macy's, it's understood that the company needs to earn your business. But when dealing with lawyers and law firms, this dynamic is often lost – for both parties. The more you step into the role of a consumer, the easier it will be for you to ensure that you get the service you want and deserve.

Make your expectations clear.

Lawyers are not mind-readers. If you go into Bicker & Bicker and spend your entire two-hour meeting blubbering about life's myriad injustices, don't expect Mr. Bicker to truly understand your expectations. By being direct with your lawyer about what you want him to do and how you want him to do it, you are more likely to be satisfied with his work.

Consider going to the law office with comments or questions in mind, such as:

- ✓ I would like to be updated on the status of my case every week. Will that work for you?
- ✓ I expect my will to be drafted by the end of the month. Is there any reason to think it'll take longer than that?
- ✓ I expect to close this real estate deal by the end of the quarter. Does that sound reasonable?
- ✓ I think this contract is a simple document to draft. Do you agree?
- ✓ I don't expect this to cost more than my initial retainer. Do you?
- ✓ I expect you to ask me before you use my retainer funds to perform any service other than what we've discussed today.
- ✓ I would prefer if you sent me drafts of all letters you send to opposing counsel before you send them.

Savvy Client Tip: You'll almost certainly bring a pen and paper into your first meeting with your lawyer. Jot down some questions or comments that you want to be sure to ask.

CHAPTER 13

Monitoring the Work Your Lawyer is Doing

G etting into the right mindset is important. But mindset alone is not enough to get what you *really* want out of your lawyer. All those lawyer jokes are out there as evidence of some basic truths: lots of people honestly believe that lawyers get rich by taking clients' money and doing nothing – and that clients are powerless because no one can effectively argue with a lawyer.

Sure, sometimes the jokes are true. Of course, there are unethical attorneys out there. But in the majority of cases, lawyers work hard for their clients. Why the jokes? Because often, clients simply do not know what the lawyer is actually doing on their cases.

Your lawyer is a *member of your team*. You can't completely check out and then expect to drop back in and complain that you didn't like the way something was handled. You need to pay attention and stay informed. In order to do that, you need to **understand what the attorney is doing**, and to **set up a system** for keeping track of what has been done.

Have your own understanding of what your lawyer is doing. We're not suggesting you go and take a class or do extensive research on the matter that you just hired your lawyer to handle. Just learn the basics of what your legal matter entails. Before you have a tonsillectomy, your doctor sits you down and tells you how he's going to perform the procedure. At the end of that conversation, no one expects that you'll be able to do it yourself. But we would expect you to have a general understanding about what surgery will entail.

In the same way, if you hire Larry Litigator to sue someone who owes you money, you should know what the basic steps in a lawsuit are.

How do you get to this understanding?

● Hit the internet. Armed with a few key phrases you can find out a lot about the trajectory of your matter. By Googling "steps in a lawsuit" or "steps to a commercial real estate closing," you should be able to piece together the basic framework of what's happening.

● This is also a good time to call in a favor from a friend who's a lawyer. Something like, "What is a lawyer's role in a real estate closing?" is a nice question to ask your friend because it's a pretty soft-ball question and doesn't involve research and doesn't put your friend on the hook for advising you.

● Check with friends or colleagues. Find someone who's been through something similar. What was the process? How long did it take? What were the steps? What did the lawyer do? Having this information can help you predict the course of action and mitigate the element of surprise.

- And of course, you should piece together this outside information with inside information. Talk to your lawyer about the kind of work he'll be doing. Gather enough information so that when he says, "I'm going to file a motion on this," or "I'm going to prep our witnesses for deposition," that you can actually picture what kind of work he'll be doing.

Keep in mind that while you're learning about what the lawyer is doing, you should be letting your newfound knowledge inform your own choices and actions as a client.

Michele once had a client engage her to handle the closing on the sale of her home. The client paid attention enough to learn that Michele had to send "the papers" to the new buyers, but the client promptly put her brain on snooze after digesting that one fact. Later, when the client changed the terms of the deal and (shock of shocks) lost the deal altogether, she neglected to even call Michele with the news. The result? Michele spent several hours drafting documents that were ultimately useless. If the client had understood the steps in the legal process and the work that was being done on her behalf, we're sure (or at least we're hopeful) Michele would have avoided spinning her wheels.

Once you have a clear idea of what your legal project is, and what role your lawyer plans to take in it, the next step is **creating and maintaining a system** that helps track accountability.

Some other good internet resources:

- http://www.nolo.com
- http://www.Legalzoom.com
- http://www.avvo.com
- http://www.findlaw.com

- http://www.abanet.org
- http://www.selfhelplaw.com
- http://www.justanswer.com
- http://www.doityourself.com
- http://www.standardlegal.com
- http://www.legaldocumentfinder.com
- http://www.co-ooperative.coop/legalservices

KEEPING TABS ON YOUR LAWYER

Step 1: Create a file.

Your file should be far thinner than your attorney's file, but it should be accurate, maintained, and accessible. In that file, you should have the following folders:

- ✓ **Correspondence:** This folder contains all communications between you and your lawyer. If you e-mail, print out the e-mails. If he sends you a letter, make sure it's in there. Notes that you take during your telephone phone or live meeting with your lawyer. In your "notes" folder, you should also keep track of any brainstorms, requests, or thoughts that you have about your case in between meetings. You may also want to include outside research that you've done on your case here.

- ✓ **Important Documents:** This folder contains copies or originals of all important documents that you've copied and turned over to your lawyer. These documents may include bills and receipts, deeds and certificates, correspondence, and other things pertaining specifically to your matter. If your lawyer is referring to them, or if you he needs an extra copy, you need to have these items easily accessible.

- ✓ **Official Legal Documents:** During the course of any legal matter, there are often official court papers, state filings, or other legally significant documents. Keeping these documents together will ensure that when you need to prove something, you won't tear your house apart in a frenzy to find the one page with the raised seal.

Step 2: Keep a log.

By taking notes on what has been done and what needs to be done, you will be able to accurately assess your attorney's performance in all phases of your matter.

Date	What comes next?	What should I be doing?
June 1: initial consultation	Phil is going to research whether I have a case and get back to me about filing a lawsuit. (two weeks)	Gathering my proof that Suzie owes my company money.
June 5: faxed Phil my proof about Suzie's debt.	Phil will call me about filing a lawsuit.	Call Phil by June 15 if I haven't heard from him.
June 15: Phil called.	Phil is going to file a complaint against Suzie. He'll draft it and get it over to me to review. (one week)	Waiting for the copy of the Complaint. Call Phil by June 21 if no complaint received yet.
June 20: Received Complaint	Process server is going to try and serve the defendant.	Nothing, just waiting.
June 22: Phil called and said that the defendant is trying to evade process.	We have to wait and see whether we can get the defendant served within the legal time frame (20 days).	Waiting. If we don't serve the defendant in time, the filing won't work.

Step 3: Use your calendar.

When it comes to monitoring the progress of any legal work, it's important that you be proactive. That means making a commitment to check up on what your lawyer is doing. Having a "no news is good news" policy isn't really the best way to get the most out of your legal representation. Of course, you should be confident that if there were a major development in your case, that your attorney would have called you – but periodic check-in phone calls can be very valuable in moving things along in between landmark moments.

JANUARY

1	2	3	4	5	6	7
					Meet with Phil @ his office.	
8	9	10	11	12	13	14
		Call Phil to see how the conference went with Judge Bonkers.				
15	16	17	18	19	20	21
			Make sure to give Phil my vacation schedule for depositions.		Make sure to get Phil copies of my incorporation docs.	
22	23	24	25	26	27	28
		Call Phil for a check-in				
29	30	31				
		Check with Belinda Bookkeeper to be sure that Suzie still hasn't paid her bill.				

CHAPTER 14

Effective Communication with Your Lawyer

Here's a little secret about attorneys: most of them *hate* talking to clients. Shocking, huh? Here you are, paying $400 an hour for your lawyer to talk to you, and he *still* doesn't want to answer the phone! How can this be? The reason attorneys often dread client calls is because clients can aggravate whatever situation the attorney is working diligently to resolve. By doing things like rambling about details, or surprising the lawyer with new information at the wrong time, clients can waste valuable time, and create bigger bills.

Another little inside-the-law-firm secret: lawyers use a standard structure for every conversation, whether it's with opposing counsel, a judge, or even a client. If you learn that structure, then you can adjust your role in the conversation accordingly.

The result? Your lawyer will take your calls on the first ring, and your bills will be lower than ever.

> **Savvy Client Tip:** Hire a lawyer as you would a babysitter: look for both competency *and* compatibility.

We have our own war stories about clients who seemed hell-bent on wasting our time and their retainer money. There was the divorce client who insisted on paying $250 an hour because her parakeet liked the sound of Elura's voice. You might think that we were thrilled to rack up billable hours by doing nothing but cooing "Polly wanna cracker?", but these kinds of conversations were always the most frustrating for us. We didn't want to bill a client for something that was non-legal and certainly not *work*. But we also didn't want to be rude, cold, or unsympathetic to our clients and their respective plights. So while we'd try to rush the ornithological part of the conversation along, we wouldn't always succeed.

> **Savvy Client Tip:** Learn the map. If you understand where your lawyer is trying to go during a conversation, you'll act more like an accelerator and less like a speed-bump.

Here's how

Think of your conversation with your lawyer as a ride on a train. You can take the local, where the ride is long, meandering and expensive. Or you can take the express, which is quick, direct and cheap.

There are five scheduled stops on the route

1. Greeting
2. Update
3. Issues
4. Assignments
5. Deadlines

Greeting

What's your lawyer trying to do: Impress you by remembering small details in your life, such as your son's first little-league game, or the name of your new wife.

What you should be doing: Bringing up, as soon as is humanly possible, any game-changing information that relates to your case. For example, in a divorce proceeding, "Mabel and I have gotten back together." Or perhaps during the drafting of your will, "My wife Mabel just got hit by an express train" – things that will drastically affect your case need to be mentioned *immediately*. Attorney-client conversations are not suspense novels. Don't save the good stuff for the end.

What you should not be doing: Treating your lawyer's small-talk as an invitation to blather on about your son's little-league team. Your lawyer doesn't care. He's just trying to be nice. And you have tons of friends who *will* care for less than $400 an hour.

> **Savvy Client Tip:** Two good questions to ask your attorney when you're reviewing a legal document are: "Is there anything out of the ordinary in this agreement?" and "If things go wrong, what would be the consequences?"

Update
What's your lawyer trying to do: Explain how your matter has progressed since the last time you've spoken.

What you should be doing: Listening and asking any questions to *clarify* what your lawyer has just said. Be on alert for legal jargon. If your attorney uses any language that you don't understand, be sure to ask for a lawyer-to-English translation!

What you should not be doing: Asking general questions and demanding legal opinions. Questions such as, "Does this mean you think that we'll win the case?" are premature during this point in the conversation. Right now, your lawyer is just trying to bring you up to speed. The real information is coming next, so stay tuned.

Issues
What's your lawyer trying to do: Explain legal or factual concerns that have arisen. For example, he may tell you a juicy tidbit that came out during a recent deposition. Or, he may share with you a recent case precedent that affects your case.

What you should be doing: Asking all questions you may have been holding back before. Do not leave this train station without fully understanding what is going on with your case.

What you should not be doing: Rushing through this part of the conversation. This is Grand Central Station of this train route. Leaving before you have a complete understanding could affect all your decisions from here on in.

Assignments
What's your lawyer trying to do: Tell you what he plans to do next, as well as what you should do next. He'll tell you what motions he plans to file, what documents he plans to draft, or what calls he plans to make. He may be asking you to gather information or documents. He may be asking you to come

up with a settlement proposal, or to make another important decision.

What you should be doing: Taking notes on what your lawyer is going to do (by using the chart "Step 2: Keep a log." on page 75). You should also be getting a clear picture of what your lawyer is asking you to do, and taking notes on all that is expected of you. You should also be telling your lawyer right away about any problems that you immediately foresee. One savvy client of ours has taken to ending this portion of our conversations with a quick "Let me say this back to you so that we can both be sure that I understand." She may have been uncomfortable with putting her own comprehension under the spotlight in this way, but the result is that with that one statement, she proved how smart she really is.

What you should not be doing: Overcomplicating things. Keeping your lawyer's instructions to you as simple as possible is the best way for you to leave the conversation understanding what he's expecting you to do.

Deadlines
What's your lawyer trying to do: Set up a realistic schedule for your next conversation and any interim dates of importance.

What you should be doing: Marking those important dates on your calendar. This is also the time to tell your lawyer that you're going on vacation for a month, or that all your company's sales records are currently in the possession of the IRS. Anything that will affect your availability is important. Bring it up.

What you should not be doing: Promising to do something by a certain date, when you *know* you'll be late. To be effective, you must be realistic. Don't promise to produce your father's death certificate by the next court date if you know that your sister has the only copy and you are embroiled in a decades-long family feud with her.

ATTORNEY-CLIENT MEETING
WITH ED THE LAWYER

Now that you've got a First-Class ticket on the Express Train, here's something to help you keep track of the ride.

Today's Date: October 15, 2012

Our next meeting date: October 30, 2012
X by telephone
☐ in person

Questions I'm planning to ask today
What happened with Annie's deposition?
Does Ed think our chances of winning this case are good?

New developments in the case
Annie Smith was deposed and did a great job.
Ed did some legal research and found out that a new court precedent would help us out a lot.

What's happening next?
Ed is going to file a "summary judgment motion," and if we win that motion, we'll win the whole case. (motion to be filed 11/15).

Assignments for me
Go to my safe-deposit box and get my divorce certificate.
Talk over a settlement amount of $30,000 with Frances.

Important date for me to keep in mind
11/1 my deposition
10/19 answers to interrogatories are due
11/1 get a check to Ed for $5,000

CHAPTER 15

How to Be a Good Client

I f you avoid doing the things that drive lawyers crazy, you'll get effective representation and the secretaries will always put your calls through on the first try. When we find ourselves at lawyers-only functions, we hear the same comment with startling frequency: "Practicing law would be great if it weren't for the clients." Hold off your initial inclination to be offended for just a minute, and follow us as we get to the bottom of this common complaint.

We've thought back on our own experiences with clients, and we've talked to lawyer friends and colleagues about their experiences. And to one degree or another, we've all worked with clients who, simply put, foul up their own representation. In fact, while preparing to write this book, we looked up "client jokes" and guess what we found? We found lists and lists of the same jokes that you've heard as "lawyer jokes," only where the *client* is the offending party.

When we were new associates, we learned quickly that some clients' calls were "NTBT" – "not to be transferred" to the partner on the case. Once, Michele made the grievous mistake of promising "I'll have Fred get right back to you" to Mrs. McGillicuddy, an NTBT client who was well-known for asking "legal" questions about how best to remodel her kitchen. To avoid being put on the client "naughty" list, learn the rules and follow them.

The Top Ten Things That Bad Clients Do

1. **Forget to wear their listening ears**. Trust us. Your lawyer doesn't *want* to charge you an extra $300 because you weren't paying attention the first two times she gave you instructions. If your lawyer tells you to send over your tax returns, *do it*! If your lawyer tells you not to call the guy suing you, *do not call him*! Lawyers are usually very clear about when they are suggesting something and when they are giving orders. You've hired this individual to represent your interests and you're probably paying through the nose for those services. Don't waste your money. Pay attention the *first* time.

2. **Have a breakdown**: *Warning*: we're about to sound really insensitive. Do not cry, hyperventilate, stomp your feet, scream, curse, or otherwise have a breakdown during an attorney-client conference. It's not that your lawyer doesn't care. It's that you're not *paying* her to care. From a

legal perspective, spending an hour blubbering is a waste of time. Lawyers are trained to do *legal* work. Your attorney understands that you are in the middle of a stressful, sensitive, important, and emotionally-charged situation. *Everyone* she represents is in the middle of a similar situation. She wants to help you resolve the *legal* aspect of your predicament in the best way possible. She does not want to waste valuable time talking you down from a ledge. We guarantee that if your lawyer were the best person to help you feel better, there would be less lawyer jokes and more psychologist jokes. If you're having a bad day, call your friend, your mom, or your shrink.

3. **Lie**: Every lawyer – male or female, litigator or transactional, big firm or solo practitioner – has had a client lie. And when clients lie, it usually causes a whole pile of related problems. By lying to him, you're making it impossible for him to do his job well. This goes for leaving out important information too. Your lawyer is the one person who will always be on your side. He *has* to be. Even if you fire him, he has to stay on your side. And, he's not even allowed to tell anyone else what you said. If you were going to the emergency room because you were having chest pains, you'd never hide the truth and tell the doc that your toe hurts. The same logic applies here. So why lie?

4. **Ask "doorknob" questions**: Don't have an hour-long estate-planning conference with your attorney, turn to leave, and with one hand on the doorknob, look back and say, "Hey Ed . . . quick question . . . I'm on trial for armed robbery later this week. Any idea what I should say to the judge?" What clients characterize as *quick* legal questions are often quite the opposite. At the beginning of your attorney-client meeting, you should have a list of all the topics you plan to discuss right in front of you. Share that list with your lawyer as early in the meeting as possible. In fact, if you have it in advance, e-mail it to her the night

before. That way, your meeting will be as efficient as possible, and when you're grasping the doorknob, the only thing you'll be saying is "Get to work!"

5. **Expect lawyers to force the horse to drink:** Lawyers are great at detailing for you all the options available in a given situation. We explain, we counsel, and we're there to help you pick up the pieces if you make a bad decision. But we do not make decisions for you. Nor do we carry out your decisions. And while we're on the subject, it's not our job to convince your business partner, your mother, or your ex-husband to see things your way. We might advise you to fire a non-compliant employee who is exposing you to liability, but please don't ask us to do the firing for you. Remember *The Godfather*? Tom Hagen was there to advise and explain. But the job of pulling literal or figurative triggers always belonged to someone else.

6. **Expect everything to be pro bono**: You have to pay your bills. It's that simple. We encourage you to scrutinize your retainer statement for accuracy, but once you're sure it's correct, *pay it*. We understand that often, clients are dealing with lawyers at particularly stressful or financially-difficult times in their lives. However, you chose to hire the lawyer. You need to pay promptly for his services. Not liking the outcome of your case is not a reason to conveniently *forget* about your bill.

7. **Obsessively call for updates.** Asking for updates is good. Becoming a stalker is not. Most of the time, it takes at least a few days for a legal matter to progress to the next step. Clients who call every single day expecting big news, are bound to be disappointed. Learning a realistic chronology of your case will help you know when to call and when to wait. During every conversation with your

lawyer, simply ask how long the next step is expected to take. Then, wait until then to call.

8. **Be an Armchair Critic**: It's not fair to complain about how your lawyer handled your matter if you don't really understand what she did. If your lawyer sends you a report, read it. If you don't understand it, call and ask questions. Put yourself in a position to accurately assess your lawyer's work – learn what's going on, ask questions, and stay informed.

9. **Set new fires**: If you're involved in a lawsuit or a major transaction, things are volatile. You've hired your attorney to resolve things. This is not the time to create new and exciting conflicts or to take actions that might affect your deal. If your attorney just spent fifteen hours hammering out the details of your child custody agreement, don't pick a fight with your ex at the drop-off until the ink is dry on the agreement.

10. **Demand unrealistic results:** While it may seem obvious to you that you were the unfortunate victim of an unjust lawsuit, the legal issues in play might be far more complex than you understand. It's your attorney's obligation to be a zealous advocate for your interests – but there are limits to what even the most persuasive attorney can do.

Savvy Client Tip: If you are tempted to be less than truthful with your lawyer, take some time to think about why. If the truth is too painful, personal, or embarrassing for you to discuss, consider telling your lawyer that more information exists, but that you're not ready to share the information.

CHAPTER 16
DIY Lawyering

We know what you're thinking. Working effectively with a lawyer is *a lot* of work. Maybe *too much* work. Maybe you should just handle this whole thing *yourself*. But as we said way back in Chapter 4, Do-it-Yourself lawyering is difficult and dangerous.

But we know that some of you just cannot resist appearing as your own counsel. So we offer you some helpful (albeit not groundbreaking) tidbits of advice and information:

- Representing yourself is called "going Pro Se" and it's done by regular people, not just criminals who've been studying law while in prison.

- You have the right to go Pro Se in every single kind of case in the entire American legal system. If you prefer to handle things yourself, you are *always* allowed to do just that.

- Despite your *right* to be your own lawyer, Pro Se litigants tend to frustrate judges, court staff, and opposing counsel, because they don't know what they're doing. Be prepared: if you do handle things on your own, you'll likely find yourself the victim of boatloads of eye-rolling, head-shaking, exasperated sighs and blatant insults from Gladys the Court Clerk and Javier the File Guy.

- Many legal matters seem simple on the surface, but have behind-the-scenes dangers just waiting to rear their ugly heads.

- Lawyers are trained to think about worst-case scenarios. In fact, the greater your attorney's ability to dream up bizarre and horrific scenarios, the better a lawyer he or she probably is. Our ability to see the glass as neither half-empty nor half-full, but rather just-on-the-edge-of-breaking-and-causing-lifelong-physical-damage is why we'll almost always advise you to leave legal work to the professionals. It's true that there are lots of legal matters that you can handle on your own with success – but don't expect your attorney to pat you on the back and encourage you to do so.

- Websites, talk shows, information booths and State Fair exhibits that purport to answer your legal questions for free are about as useful as (fill in the blank with your favorite idiom). The people behind them are in the business of practicing law and they are trying to drum up new business by giving you half an answer and telling you to call them at the office in the morning for the other half.

- Use free legal information in a wise way. For example, let's say that you've been the owner of Harrison's Custom Hat and Dill Pickle Shop for ten years, and ever since your appearance on *America's Best-Dressed Pickleteers* last season, business is booming. You've talked to some smart entrepreneurs, your third cousin who's in law school, and your Aunt Polly (the originator of all your pickle secrets) and have decided to form a Limited Liability Company. Hitting the internet is a fantastic next step. Look up the sites where you see templates. Make notes of all the issues you will need to think about, the questions you have, and the choices available to you. If the sites you visit are helpful, you should be able to foresee future financial dealings, structural changes, distribution of profits, partnership opportunities, and management schemes. If you use legal information in this wise way, you'll be able to figure out quite a bit before bringing in your lawyer— and your hard work will save you time and money.

- Be careful with forms. There are zillions of websites out there that offer legal forms for download. Some are free, some are cheap, some are expensive. Sometimes, downloadable forms are fabulous DIY tools. Other times, they are a portal into the world of Eternal Legal Regrets. The most common problem with downloadable forms is that many are too generic to be useful. Many forms, such as wills and incorporation documents, have state-specific requirements. What will happen if you download a Nebraska will and try to use it in Michigan? Maybe it'll work. Maybe it won't. The problem is that you won't know what the problem is until it's a problem.

- Remember that often, the best person to tell you what a lawyer could do for you isn't a lawyer at all. Talking to people who have been *clients* can be far more helpful in many situations. For example, let's say you've just invented the *Binkmaster 3000*, which is bound to revolutionize pacifier-sterilization for busy moms all over America, and you think you're ready to hire a patent lawyer . . . but you're just not sure. Instead of consulting with fifteen patent lawyers, you could go to www. mominventors. com and get some useful information by connecting with other inventors. Asking people with situations similar to yours questions like, "At what point did you hire your lawyer?" or, "What exactly did your lawyer do for you?" can be extremely helpful.

- There is a great deal of information available to you, for free, right at your local courthouse. If you are involved in the kind of business where there's likely to be frequent litigation in your future, you may do very well by taking the time to learn the ropes. Elura's Uncle Frank is a professional commercial landlord. And he's the kind of guy who loves to jump in and get his hands dirty. Whether the matter at hand is a clogged pipe or a rent dispute, Uncle Frank would rather handle it himself than pay a premium to some so-called "professional." Early on in his landlordhood, Uncle Frank invested some time in learning how landlord-tenant court works. He went down to the courthouse, had lunch with the clerks, met a few lawyers, and observed a few cases. Now, whenever he needs to sue a tenant, he's able to handle the entire matter himself with as much success as a seasoned attorney. If you have the kind of business that will likely bring up repeated and similar legal issues (landlord-tenant relations, unpaid invoices, traffic tickets), consider using the Uncle Frank model. You may save some money and gain valuable legal knowledge in the process.

So now that we've beaten you over the head with our warnings and advice, we can sleep at night. If you choose to take matters into your own hands, remember to allot adequate time for your legal matter, and to be patient with yourself. Remember that there are many people, books, and websites out there to help you. Be reasonable with your expectations, and if things ever seem to spiral out of control, call your lawyer immediately.

Now go forth and lawyer at your own risk.

(For a list of some DIY-Lawyering Websites, see "Some other good internet resources:" on page 73.)

CHAPTER 17

Why Do Lawyers Talk That Way?

One of the main reasons so many people dislike talking to lawyers (aside from being billed $400 an hour to do so) is that the *way* lawyers talk tends to alienate regular people. From the jargon or "legal-ese", to the wishy-washy non-committal answers, to the seemingly never-ending questions, lawyerspeak can frustrate and annoy even the most patient client. You may wonder why lawyers don't just decide to speak *English*. The truth? We can't. Really. Law school teaches us a new way of thinking and speaking, and we are literally *unable* to go back to our old ways.

But we're not using the jargon to alienate, annoy, or frustrate you. We're not *trying* to overcomplicate things, and we're not *trying* to over-lawyer things. We are simply trying to communicate *accurately*. When your carpenter uses a different hammer for each of fifteen different sized-nails, you usually don't complain. When your plumber brings in a toolbox filled with two hundred wrenches, you don't roll your eyes – you simply assume that *he's* the professional and he knows why he needs

I COULD KNOCK OFF THE LEGAL JARGON, BUT, THEN I'D HAVE **NOTHING**, TO SAY!

all those tools. For lawyers, words are *our* tools. You hire us to speak on your behalf. You hire us to draft agreements. You hire us to tell you exactly how to proceed in sensitive situations. It's important that we are accurate and precise with the language we use.

So if you feel like your attorney is intentionally talking over your head, or giving you the run-around, it might just be that she's using a communication style that works well for her, and that she doesn't realize its effect on you.

Professional jargon is a fact of life

Here's the thing: *all* professionals use jargon. Doctors, bankers, financial advisors, pyschologists, engineers—*everybody* who has specialized knowledge. They learn and use specialized language on a daily basis among people who understand it. They deal with problems that, despite being uniquely challenging for us, become *routine* to them. When your sister the clarinetist laces the dinner conversation with references to Mozart's chromatic grace-note figures, you think it's cute. But somehow, when your lawyer launches into a discussion of *force-majeure* clauses, you feel intimidated and threatened. People with specialized knowledge can become naturally disconnected from the regular English-speaking public. But we all *need* specialists to help us in different areas of our lives – so it's important that we deal with the jargon problem, head-on.

Admit when you don't understand

The single most important thing you can do to stop professional jargon from interfering with your relationship with your professional is to create conversational speed-bumps. Any time your lawyer (or doctor, CPA, engineer, or clarinetist, for that matter) uses a word that you don't understand, *speak up*! Stop the conversation, ask for clarification, and resume only when you're certain that you and your professional are on the same page. Admitting that you don't understand is not a sign of stupidity – it's a sign of intelligence. Remember – your lawyer isn't using the legal jargon to seem superior (that's what the monogrammed French-cuffs and bowties are for) – he's using the jargon because *that's how he talks*. Remember—you can be his envoy back to the world of regular English-speakers by simply reminding him that you aren't familiar with the term "*pendente lite*."

When our friend Eva, a world-famous neurologist, was about to buy her first home, she spoke with her mortgage broker nearly every day. During their conversations, her broker would suggest that Eva purchase different financial products, often using inside-mortgage-industry lingo. Good 'ol Eva stopped her broker at every reference to "balloon payments," "ARMs," or "no-doc loans" to demand a full and complete definition of each. Because Dr. Eva was confident enough to demand clarification of terms, she armed herself with the appropriate knowledge to make wise choices about her mortgage. And you don't have to be a brain surgeon to be smart enough to act just like Eva. If you're ever feeling like a conversation is going over your head, with any professional, demand clarification. And if doing so makes you feel inferior in some way, just throw in some jargon from your own workplace and see how the professional reacts.

Why you can't get a straight answer

Clients often perceive lawyers as giving wishy-washy, non-committal answers. If you ask your lawyer, "Do you think I'll win my case?" and she answers, "Absolutely! You're bound to get a million-dollar judgment!", you should either lay off the Ambien, or get a new lawyer. Lawyers are trained to be precise with their language – and that means staying away from absolutes. You will rarely hear a lawyer say "YES" or "NO" without adding some caveat. Because outcomes in law are never completely predictable, it would be unprofessional and cavalier for a lawyer to ever promise a particular outcome in your case. You're more likely to hear phrases like "in a reasonable time frame" or "cautiously optimistic" or "the odds are in your favor" – which are understandably frustrating in their ambiguity, but are ultimately accurate. And accuracy with our predictions and advice is our primary goal.

The same goal of precision goes for all the "heretofores" and "notwithstandings" in written agreements. Lawyers try to write contracts that take subjective interpretation out of the equation. It's our desire to make every clause absolutely airtight that leads to the perception that the quickest way to overcomplicate anything is to bring in a lawyer. Keep in mind that usually, no one pays much attention to the wording of legal agreements until something goes wrong. Unlike the parties who have signed the contract, your lawyer is trained to think about the Dark Side, right from the start. She's not trying to punch holes in your genius idea just for the fun of it, or to make you feel bad – she's trying to anticipate what could go wrong so she can protect you. And in the unfortunate event that things do fall apart, that well-drafted, air-tight document will protect you.

"WHEN I NOD MY HEAD… YOU HIT IT!"

Jargon in sheep's clothing

If the "herewiths" and "wherefors" weren't enough for you, there are lots of words that sound like regular English that are actually legal terms of art. For example, the words "best efforts", "best evidence," and "fair use" may sound benign, but they actually have rather precise legal meanings. Don't worry – it's not your job to learn all this lawyer-lingo; it's simply your job as a savvy client to know that it exists. It's a good idea to ask your lawyer to walk you through *any* contract – whether he's drafted it, or whether another attorney has – and explain to you what you are signing *before* you put your John Hancock in ink. He can explain any legal terms that aren't immediately obvious – and he can (and should!) explain the *implications* of each clause.

CHAPTER 18

How to Complain About Your Lawyer

There are times when you *know* that your lawyer screwed up. If, for instance, your lawyer showed up in court drunk, used your retainer funds to go to Disneyland, or slept with opposing counsel, we invite you to skip down to Chapter 19, "When to Call the Ethics Board."

If, on the other hand, you find yourself in the not-uncommon position of just being miffed with your attorney, then read on. Something has annoyed you, either a lot or a little . . . and you're on the road to Complaintville.

To ensure that you get the best result possible from your soon-to-be-aired grievance, it's important that you properly evaluate and articulate the basis of your complaint. Otherwise, you can be sure that your First-Class ticket to Complaintville will have an indefinite layover in Frustrationland.

Step 1: Never complain about the result. Always complain about the process.

An attorney has one obligation: to represent you zealously to the best of his or her ability. Lawyers are not obligated to ensure that you get the particular legal result for which you'd hoped. In this regard, lawyers are like massage therapists. You pay for the process, not the result. If you're still stressed out at the end of a four-hour-hour massage, you may choose not to return to Zelda's House of Hands ... but you still owe the $400.

It's process that you buy, not the end result. So a good complaint will be about how the lawyer's bad actions led to a result that is making you unhappy. When articulating a complaint, you should always point to a cause-effect relationship between what your lawyer should have done and what has made you unhappy.

Savvy Client Tip: If you ended up with a result that is very different from what you expected, schedule a conference with your lawyer for the sole purpose of discussing the outcome. Knowledge is power. You probably can't change the result, but you can learn from the experience.

Step 2: Think about the point of your complaint.

Before you start throwing rotten tomatoes at your lawyer's office, you need to decide what result you're trying to achieve.

There are four basic possibilities:

1. **Improve your working relationship with your lawyer.** If you're feeling like you're getting the coach treatment when you've paid for first class, a targeted complaint can be very effective. The most important aspects of your complaint are **directness** and **specificity.** First, call your lawyer and be direct. Tell her that you're unhappy with the length of time it takes her to return phone calls, and that you expect all calls to be returned within 24 hours. Explain that last-minute scheduling is inconvenient for you, and request that all appointments made three days in advance. Remind him that you don't check e-mail daily, and demand that you be telephoned with case updates. Don't be afraid to voice your complaint. Do be sure to give your lawyer specific guidance about what you expect. After you're made your demands clear, following up with an e-mail or letter is also a great way to remind your lawyer that you were serious. And if your conversation with counsel doesn't end with some version of "Okay, Bob, I'll promise to do that in the future," you should start shopping around for new representation.

2. **Get the lawyer to change what he's doing on your case.** If you are unhappy with your lawyer's courtroom demeanor, writing-style, or general professionalism, you need to speak up. Remember, you've hired her to speak on your behalf; if you don't like what she's saying, it's time to complain. Have an open and honest discussion with your lawyer about your dissatisfaction. Be direct and specific, and detail how you think she should have proceeded. Keep in mind, though, that your lawyer may have a different opinion about what the most effective course of action was. While you may have preferred a more aggressive approach to your case, your attorney may have a legitimate reason for the way in which she proceeded. What you may perceive as a particular lawyering style

may actually be strategy. Stay direct and focused, but open-minded. If you find that philosophical or strategic differences are daily occurrences, consider ending your relationship with your lawyer. But give your lawyer a chance – she may be doing things differently than you would have – but those differences may well be the reason you hired her in the first place.

3. **Get rid of this lawyer, and get somebody else.** If you have decided that it's time to break up with your attorney, then you need to stay focused on that goal. Treat this firing like a bank robbery: get in and out as quickly as possible, and try to keep the talking to a minimum. The longer the conversation, the more your lawyer will try to convince you to stay on as a client. If you're beyond that stage, then take control of the conversation and be firm. And don't forget to request that all files pertaining to your matter and any unused retainer funds be immediately forwarded to you at your lawyer's expense. Be aware, however, that if you owe your lawyer any money for work he has already done, he is entitled to have an "attorney's lien" on your files (which allows him to hold those files hostage) until you are paid up.

4. **Get rid of this clown and cause a ruckus.** In the unfortunate event that you find yourself on the receiving end of serious attorney misconduct, there are lots of avenues for you to voice your displeasure. First, call go to your computer and Google "[your state name], "ethics" and "professional responsibility." The first thing that comes up should be your state's ethics board. More on that in the next chapter. It's the first place to take a major complaint. Some states maintain an insurance fund that protects clients in the event of serious misconduct. Be sure to inquire about compensation when you speak with the ethics board. If you're still not satisfied, you can always call your

state's Attorney General's office. Then, call your lawyer, fire her, and demand a quick refund.

And always remember to use complaining the way you would use nutmeg. Too little, it'll have no effect. Too much, and it'll mess things up and leave a bitter taste in everyone's mouth. When necessary, complain enough to be noticed, but not enough to be a pest.

> **Savvy Client Tip:**
>
> Some people, including lawyers, are just plain jerks. If your lawyer seems to get off on making himself seem important by making you feel incompetent, GET RID OF HIM! Good lawyers WANT their clients to understand why and how they're doing what they're doing.

Savvy Client Tip: Make friends with your lawyer's secretary. That way, you can check in about minor details on the days when you need some reassurance. And the secretary won't bill you!

CHAPTER 19

When to Call the Ethics Board

Certain things speak for themselves. If your attorney skipped town, arrived to court tweaked up on crystal meth, stole your car, or cursed out the judge, it's pretty clear that you should call the ethics board. But what about when your attorney was chronically late to court? Or when she took a month to return your phone message?

Despite all the jokes, lawyers are expected to adhere to a pretty detailed and strict code of legal ethics. Lawyers that break the rules can be disciplined in a variety of ways. Depending on the severity of the misconduct, the offender could be fined, lose his law license, or even be criminally prosecuted. You don't need to understand the ins and outs of the various codes of professional responsibility. Just go with your gut. If you believe that your lawyer has acted badly enough that you want to start a big ruckus, you need to contact the ethics board.

But it's important that you understand what you are doing when you make this kind of complaint. Calling the committee that oversees attorney conduct in your state is *not* the legal equivalent of calling the Better Business Bureau. Making an ethical complaint against a lawyer is **not** simply a way to air your grievances. Ethical complaints are serious business. Lawyers that are found to have violated the rules of professional conduct face serious consequences—so make sure that your complaint is appropriate before making the call.

Who do you call?

Every state has a different name for the group of people who oversees attorney conduct. To find out the name for the group in your state,

Google "[your state name], 'ethics' and 'professional responsibility'." Usually, the first or second website listed will bring you to a governmental or quasi-governmental body that polices attorney ethics.

What will happen after you call?

Most likely, your complaint will be treated much like a criminal investigation would be treated. Someone will investigate (which means that you'll probably have to tell your story to a bunch of people and send them a bunch of supporting documentation), and eventually, someone will decide whether the attorney needs to be disciplined. You may be asked to testify, fill out affidavits, or meet personally with an investigator.

Like a criminal investigation, attorney ethical violation investigations are really matters between the investigator and the perpetrator of misconduct. That means that no one will be reporting in to you to update you on the status of Slimy the Sleazeball's disbarment.

What will happen to the lawyer?

He may be censured, fined, suspended or disbarred.

What will not happen?

The ethics board will not change the outcome in your court case. So, for example, let's say that Donald McDoofus, Esq. represented you when you were being sued for a breach of contract. You had a great defense, but Donald arrived to court, drunk as a skunk, and as a result, you lost the whole case. Even if Donald is disbarred, it would not automatically mean a do-over for your case. You might be able to appeal your case, but that, as they say, is "a whole nother matter."

Will you ever be compensated for your attorney's wrongdoing?

Maybe. It all depends on the exact circumstances of your case. Some states have special insurance funds that compensate victims of legal misconduct or malpractice. Sometimes, you'd need to file a legal malpractice action against your lawyer (yes, there are lawyers who specialize in suing their fellow lawyers for legal misconduct). If you need to be compensated for your lawyer's misconduct, the best thing you can do is (gulp) hire another lawyer.

What about the money that you have left on your retainer?

Theoretically, your retainer money is like a bank account. The money you paid sits in your lawyer's trust account, and he only moves it over into his personal account as he works on your case. So, if you pre-paid $5,000, and your attorney only worked 2 hours on your case before becoming disbarred, you are entitled to get a refund for all unused funds. This might be a problem when you're dealing with a lawyer who is in hot water because of an ethical investigation. However, don't just assume that your money is gone. Call the ethics board, and ask them how to proceed.

CHAPTER 20

The Big Finish

Well, you did it. By finishing this book, you've demonstrated a real desire to be proactive in your relationship with your attorney. There's only one thing left to do: GO FORTH AND PUT THOSE LESSONS TO WORK! You've got templates above, a glossary below, and official *How To Talk To Your Lawyer* know-how to shift the balance of power in your favor. We're not saying that by doing everything we say, you'll be a good client . . . aw heck, yes we are!! Now get going!

Savvy Client Tip: If you're having trouble paying your legal bills, consider asking for a payment plan. Attorneys are often willing to collect over time if they feel comfortable that you won't skip out on their bills.

GLOSSARY

Acronyms for statutes that they'll throw around as if you understand (ERISA, CEPA, RICO, etc): Some federal laws (or "statutes") have very long names, and we quick-talking lawyers give them nicknames. We do it because it sounds slick. But here's a list of the commonly-used ones, so that you can share in our collective slickness:

ERISA: The Employee Retirement Income Security Act: This protects people's pensions from various shenanigans by the pension administrator.

CEPA: The Conscientious Employee Protection Act (also known as the "Whistleblower" law). This law gives protection to people who are fired from their jobs after they complain or "blow the whistle" on their employer for some wrongdoing.

OSHA: The Occupational Safety and Health Act: This law requires employers to keep workplaces safe from things like dangerous chemicals and falling anvils.

RICO: The Racketeer-Influenced and Corrupt Organization Act. This is the law that gets used for organized crime cases. It's a complicated criminal statute that is designed to tie together bunches of crimes, such as money-laundering, and make them into one giant legal mess for the defendant and one giant season of *The Sopranos* for the rest of us.

Admissible: Lots of information changes hands during a lawsuit. But only some of that information will end up in front of a judge or jury. When information is "admissible," it means that it's allowed to get into the courtroom. Keep in mind, though – just because something is admissible does not mean that it will end up in the courtroom.

Adversary: The "other lawyer." In a lawsuit, the lawyer who represents the other party is your lawyer's "adversary." The "other guy" in your lawsuit—the one who hired the adversary – is your "opponent."

Attorney/Legal Counsel/Lawyer/Esq: Here's something you shouldn't waste one kilowatt of brainpower on. These are all synonyms. Yes, you'll find some smartasses out there who have researched a distinction stemming from ye days of olde . . . but these days, they all mean the same thing.

Attorneys' fees: This one seems self-explanatory, doesn't it? Well, while "attorneys' fees" might simply refer to the money someone pays a lawyer for legal work, the phrase often has a more sinister meaning. Saying that someone may be responsible for "attorneys' fees" typically implies that the person paying is actually paying for the other person's lawyer. In litigation, when one party does something very wrong, or when someone wins certain kinds of cases, the court may order that the losing party pays the attorneys' fees of the winning party. This kind of double-whammy is also known as "fee-shifting." It doesn't happen very often, but when it does, you'll certainly hear about it.

Cause of Action: Just substitute "thing that you could sue about" for this term. When someone sees a car accident and tells you that "you've got a lawsuit there," what they should actually be saying is, "you've got a cause of action there." It just doesn't sound as sexy.

Cease & Desist: Lawyerspeak for "knock it off!" If you're talking about a "Cease and Desist Order," it means that a court has ordered someone to knock it off or else be held in contempt of court, which is pretty serious business. If you're talking about a "Cease and Desist Letter," then it's simply a person or business' way of saying, "knock it off or else I'll sue you!" which is less serious, because it has no official legal function. Anyone can write a Cease and Desist Letter, but lawyers are especially good at it, since we know all the intimidating lingo.

The "clerk": This is like the "shalom" of legal jargon. It means everything. Inside a law firm, a "clerk" usually means the low man on the totem pole – often an intern, or a law-school student who is working part-time. Inside a courthouse, there's the "court clerk," who is a non-lawyer that has a top-level administrative position within the court. There's also the judge's "law clerk" (sometimes called a "law secretary"), who is a lawyer and who acts like the judge's right-hand man, by communicating with lawyers, doing legal research, and talking things over with the judge. None of these folks should be confused with the "county clerk" or similar titles that refer to political or quasi-political governmental figures that handle various official documents and filings. In any environment where there are lots of files, there are usually "file clerks" also, which typically refers to people whose job is . . . well, to file.

Copyright: A right, granted by the government, to allow someone to have the right to copy, show, or perform pieces of music, art, or writing (but not ideas).

Copyright/Trademark infringement: Illegal use or copying of something (like a piece of artwork or a name of a business).

This is what you'd sue someone for if they "stole" your song or if they made illegal copies of a DVD.

Damages: You'll hear this word used in two different ways. Sometimes, "damages" will describe the way a person was harmed by another person. For example, when you drop your neighbor's Fabregé egg, you cause damage, and your neighbor has "damages." Sometimes, lawyers will refer to "damages" as something a winning plaintiff gets. So Randy might be awarded "damages" by the court when Edna damaged his egg, causing Randy to suffer "damages."

Deposition: You've definitely seen this on TV or in the movies. Several lawyers are sitting around a conference table while people testify. The questions are a lot like what would be asked in a courtroom, but there's no judge and no jury. On TV, the person testifying always ends up crying or blurting out some juicy secret. In real life, depositions are incredibly boring, take a very long time, and cost everyone a fortune. Depositions are the part of the discovery process whereby each side learns a little about the other side's story.

"Diary it": Most lawyers use a task-management system called "diarying." Practicing law requires a lawyer to juggle tons of dates and deadlines, and the easiest way to keep track of everything is by using a daily calendar (also called a "diary") on which upcoming matters of importance are scheduled. So if your lawyer says, "You should've received your incorporation papers from the State. I'll diary a call to the Secretary of State for Monday," it means that he's scheduled a phone call onto his calendar that he'll be making on Monday. The reason your lawyer doesn't use the word "calendar" (when that's exactly what the rest of the non-lawyer world would say), is because "calendar" refers to the Court's schedule, not the lawyer's schedule.

Discovery (and related discovery/litigation words): It's cute that lawyers use this word, which sounds all mysterious and fun, to mean something that is . . . well . . . not. A more accurate term would be "aggravation period" or perhaps "the expensive, stressful, hunt for documents." "Discovery" refers to the time period after a lawsuit is filed, but before the trial begins. During discovery, both sides turn over all sorts of information to each other, witnesses are interviewed, depositions are taken, questions are exchanged, motions are made, and settlement is discussed. The more complex the case, the longer and more annoying the discovery promises to be.

Disposition: This sounds a lot like "deposition," but means something completely different. The "disposition" in a case refers to the final court order in a particular lawsuit. When the court is finished with a case, it takes the docket number off its itinerary and "disposes" of the case. Every case has a final "disposition" from the perspective of the court. The disposition could be a judgment for either party, a dismissal of the case, a final injunction, etc.

Due diligence: A fancy way of saying "doing your homework on someone." Also known as "background research," "getting the lay of the land" or "getting up to speed," "due diligence" refers to the process of gathering and evaluating relevant information prior to making some kind of deal or decision. It sounds much more lawyerly and bill-worthy to say, "we're performing due diligence on the Pensky deal" than it does to say, "we have to go through Mr. Pensky's old bills to see if he owes anyone any money."

Indemnification: The legal way to make someone else pay for something that was his fault in the first place. For example, you got rear-ended while stopped at a traffic light. When you got hit, you hit the car in front of you, causing $500 in damages. The guy you hit sues you and you pay $500. This whole mess wasn't your fault, so you sue the guy who hit you, since it was his fault, he'll pay you $500 in indemnification to make up for what you paid out. When the whole mess was someone else's fault, you'll seek "indemnification." When only part of the mess was someone else's fault, you'll seek "contribution."

Injunction: A court order that makes someone stop doing something.

Matter: The thing your attorney is working on for you. We with law degrees like to be very precise about our language. Everyone else may say "case," but that wouldn't be exactly correct for non-litigation. At firms, clients are given identification numbers, and then each "matter" is given its own identification number.

Motions: During the course or a lawsuit, one side or the other will need, periodically, to ask the court to do something. The way that the "asking" is done is by "making a motion." The purpose motions can be almost anything – from forcing one person to turn over documents, to clarifying what a particular clause in a contract means. Motions are "made" by filing a bunch of papers that explain why the person filing needs the court to intervene.

Patent: The same thing as a copyright, but for an invention or formula.

Per Diem: This is Latin (which is why lawyers love to use it) for "for each day." For example, you might be charged interest at a rate of 7% per diem, which means the interest will be compounded each day. You can be sure, however, that your lawyer's fees will be calculated per hour, and not per diem.

Pleadings: All the official paperwork that goes with a lawsuit.

Power of Attorney: This refers to both a power and a document that creates the power. When one person has "the power of attorney" for another person, it means that the person with the power can legally act on behalf of the person giving the power. It's the legal authority to stand in someone else's shoes. Your lawyer can have "power of attorney" for you, which would allow him to appear in court without you having to be there. Or your friend/sister/colleague can have "power of attorney" for you and sign documents, or otherwise represent you on your behalf. How do you get to have the power? You have a lawyer draft a form called . . . you guessed it . . . a "power of attorney" form.

Precedent: Cases that have come before your case that have established rules that later courts must follow.

Remedy: Things that you can win in a lawsuit. "Damages" (money) are one kind of remedy, but there are also other kinds of remedies, such as injunctions or other court orders.

Representations: The rest of the world uses the word "said" for this one, as in "He said that the ink cartridge I bought would fit in my printer!" Translated into Legalese, it would be, "The store manager made a representation to my client that this was the correct cartridge for my client's printer." Because certain kinds of statements are legally important, we need a stronger-sounding word to describe them.

Sanctions: A court issues "sanctions" when someone (either one of the lawyers or one of the parties) has really messed up. Sanctions are court orders to pay a specific amount of money to the court as punishment for bad behavior.

Servicemark: The same thing as a trademark, but for a service.

Settlement: Always a good thing, "settlement" usually refers to the agreement that parties to a lawsuit have come to for resolution of their dispute. Of course, if you're talking about a transaction, "settlement" can also refer to the process by which property changes hands (also known as the "closing").

Statute of Limitations: The time period during which you are allowed to file a lawsuit about a particular event. Usually, you will have 1-6 years (depending on the type of case) from the time when you've been harmed in which you are permitted to file a lawsuit. If you wait longer than the statute allows, you've lost your chance.

Stay: Think dog commands. In legal terms, "stay" can be a noun that refers to a court order that makes another court order "hold still" for a little while. So if Judge Flanders ordered you to shut down your peanut-shelling factory immediately, Judge Smithson might issue a "stay" that would allow you to stay in business for a little while longer.

Trademark: A right, granted by the government, to allow someone to have the right to use a particular name for a business or product.

Warranties: Things that people or businesses say (or write) that they are legally obligated to stand behind. It's a complex area of law, but if you picture a salesman promising, "I guarantee that this car will go from 0 to 60 in 3. 1 seconds" – you've pictured a warranty.

Whitepaper: Basically, a report or term-paper, just like you wrote in middle school. The only difference is that it's been written by a grownup for the specific purpose of helping someone make a decision about something.

About the Authors

Michele Sileo, Esq.

All her life, Michele had heard that she'd make a great lawyer. Little girls who grew up in Bensonhurst, Brooklyn didn't usually become lawyers – but that didn't stop Michele. After graduating from New York Law School, Michele set out to fight for child support on behalf of New York City's Administration for Children's Services. When she finished with the deadbeats of New York City, Michele represented hospitals and doctors in medical malpractice lawsuits for the law firm of Martin Clearwater & Bell, LLP.

For the past decade, as the owner of Lawyer Up, Michele has used her street-smarts and sassy style to make law understandable and useful for professionals and law students alike.

Michele currently lives in Staten Island, New York, with her husband, N.Y.P.D. Captain James Grant, seven year-old Lieutenant James, and three year-old Chief Olivia. In any fleeting free time she finds, Michele does what all working mothers do – the laundry.

Elura Nanos, Esq.

A fourth-generation entrepreneur, Elura broke the family mold by making school her first career, studying African-American literature, classical music, and law. As a newly-minted member of the New York bar, Elura worked as a trial lawyer in the child abuse and neglect division of New York City's Administration for Children's Services. Later, she rounded out her legal experience by practicing commercial litigation and family law at Blank Rome, LLP, in Cherry Hill, New Jersey.

When Elura could no longer resist the lure of being her own employer, she founded Lawyer Up, and has never looked back. Now, she travels the globe (or at least the neighborhood) showing people that legal expertise doesn't require pinstripes, bow-ties, or jargon.

Elura lives with her very patient husband and two snuggly kids in Cherry Hill, New Jersey. Plate-spinning is a way of life for Elura, who also finds time to serve as a board member of several charitable educational organizations. In addition to being a lawyer and entrepreneur, Elura is a piccolo-playing lover of audiobooks, Mozart, and movies about prison, and a hater of crawling plants, war documentaries, and raisins.

www.LetsLawyerUp.com

About Lawyer Up

Elura and Michele met as overwhelmed law students, bonded as practicing attorneys, and joined forces to bring their unique talents to the law students of New York. The vibrant and down-to-earth duo was an overnight hit with the law-school set, and

Lawyer Up was born. Now in its ninth year, Lawyer Up works with law students nationwide to help them ace their courses with less stress.

Elura and Michele have taken their talent for breaking down tough legal concepts into tasty, bite-sized pieces to an even broader audience. Working with business owners, professionals, and anyone who wants to learn law, the best friends and business partners help everyone "Lawyer Up" by breaking down barriers between attorneys and clients across the country.

For more information about how you can Lawyer Up with Elura and Michele, we invite you to visit **www.LetsLawyerUp.com.**

About Right Brain Ventures

At Right Brain Ventures, we've witnessed – over and over again – how systematic planning, knowledge of business financials and self-confidence contributes to building successful businesses and personal wealth. But we've also seen how difficult it can be for owners of small businesses to find practical, intuitive business growth tools – and resources they can trust.

Right Brain Ventures was founded to bridge that gap. RBV products help link our wonderfully creative "right brain" entrepreneurial clients with the "left brain" systems that can help them achieve their dreams.

We're pleased to introduce the "How to Talk to Your..." series with this fun and practical guide to how to get the most out of your relationship with your lawyer. As business owners themselves, lawyers Elura Nanos and Michele Sileo are perfectly equipped to empower fellow entrepreneurs by shining a light on the attorney-client mystique.

Watch for other volumes, coming soon!